Woodcarving

Everett Ellenwood

www.FoxChapelPublishing.com

ISBN 978-1-56523-366-9

Publisher's Cataloging-in-Publication Data

Ellenwood, Everett.

 Woodcarving / Everett Ellenwood. -- 1st ed. -- East Petersburg, PA :
Fox Chapel Publishing, c2008.

  p. ; cm.
  (Kidcrafts)
  ISBN: 978-1-56523-366-9

  Summary: All you need are sharp tools, a piece of wood, and
an imagination to create your own works of art by carving wood.
Seven woodcarving projects include all the information you need
for success, including tool lists, materials and supply lists, skill lists,
and step-by-step photographic instructions especially designed for
kids.

  1. Wood-carving--Juvenile literature. 2. Wood-carving--
Technique--Juvenile literature. 3. Wood-carving--Patterns.
4. [Wood-carving. 5. Woodwork. 6. Handicraft.] I. Title. II. Series.

TT199.7 .E454 2008
736/.4--dc22   2008

To learn more about the other great books from Fox Chapel Publishing, or to find a retailer near
you, call toll free 800-457-9112 or visit us at www.FoxChapelPublishing.com.

Note to Authors: We are always looking for talented authors to write new books in our area of
woodworking, design, and related crafts. Please send a brief letter describing your idea to
Acquisition Editor, 1970 Broad Street, East Petersburg, PA 17520.

First Printing: July 2008

Printed in China

Table of Contents

Look What You Can Carve

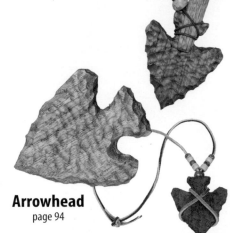

Here's All You Need to Get Started

Knife

Wood

Sandpaper

INTRODUCTION
How to Use This Book

Woodcarving is a fun hobby you can do for the rest of your life. Anyone can learn to carve. All you need are sharp tools, a piece of wood, and an imagination.

As long as there has been wood and people, there has been woodcarving. Every country in the world has a history of woodcarving. Cavemen were likely the first carvers, using sharp stones to make wooden tools for digging and spears for hunting.

People have always wanted to make and decorate wood items. This book shows how you, too, can have fun making items with wood.

Before you tackle the projects in this book, be sure to read about the types of wood you should use (Chapter 1), the readily available supplies that are helpful (Chapter 2), and the tools you may want and how to use them safely (Chapter 3).

The seven woodcarving projects in this book (Chapter 4) are ordered from easy to more difficult. Complete the projects in order so you can learn and build upon your woodcarving skills.

Each project includes the information you need to complete it successfully:

- A list of tools visually shows you what you need.

- Material and supply lists help you gather the supplies you will use.

- Skill lists show you what techniques to review.

- Photographic step-by-step instructions show you exactly how to succeed in making the project.

By working through the book, you will learn to transfer patterns, measure and mark, drill holes, saw shapes, use carving tools, sand and finish wood, and sharpen and care for your tools. In addition, you will end up with a variety of fun projects you will be proud to show others.

Follow the instructions in this book, and you will see how much fun it is to create your own works of art by carving wood.

Note to Adults

This book has been written to help young people learn how to carve wood. It offers exercises and projects that build skills and allows kids to create things they can be proud of.

To test a child's maturity and dexterity, have the child try the soap-carving project on page 70. In making the soap boat, young carvers will learn how to lay out the project and safely use various simple tools. How they use the soap-carving tools will give you a good idea of how they would handle sharp tools. If you believe they can stay focused and have the dexterity to safely use sharp tools with your supervision, they should be able to progress to carving some simple wood projects.

Although this book covers a variety of tools and options that can make carving easier, each project requires only a few simple tools. Practice exercises are included with the chapters on supplies and tools (Chapters 2 and 3), and the skills are used throughout the book. This structure allows kids to proceed with a project if they've already learned the skill or review the practice exercises if the skill still needs work.

I recommend carving only for children over age 10, unless a younger child has a high degree of maturity and dexterity. Carving wood requires razor-sharp tools and can be dangerous if not done properly.

Whenever young people are carving wood, I recommend at least one adult for each child to ensure the kids are following all safety procedures and properly using the tools.

If done properly, woodcarving can be a safe and rewarding experience. Give kids an opportunity to find the joy of creating something in wood. Who knows—you may want to join them.

CHAPTER 1
All About Wood

A deciduous tree.

You probably already know that trees provide wood to build homes and food to nourish us. They are the oldest and largest of all living plants. Trees also help control erosion, provide shelter and food for wildlife, and add beauty to the world with their different colors and shapes.

The many types of trees around us provide a variety of wood that can be carved. So let us take a closer look at this material you will be carving. You will want to learn as much as you can about wood before you start, because the more you know about wood, the more effectively you'll be able to use it.

Coniferous trees.

Hardwood or Softwood?

Trees are divided into two categories: hardwoods and softwoods. Though you may think hardwoods must be harder than softwoods, it is not always true. Woodworkers use the terms hardwood and softwood to describe the type of tree wood comes from, not the hardness of the wood itself. Hardwood comes from deciduous trees. These trees have leaves that fall off in autumn. Softwood comes from conifers. These trees have needles, like those found on pine trees, which stay on all year.

Whether wood is hardwood or softwood, it's the weight of a dry piece of wood that determines how hard or easy the wood is to carve. The more a piece of wood weighs, the harder it will be to carve. The weight of wood is directly proportional to its hardness.

Anatomy of a Tree

Whatever type of wood you choose, how a tree grows determines how you carve the wood. All trees have three main parts: the roots, the trunk, and the crown.

The roots grow into the ground and keep the tree erect. They also absorb water and minerals from the ground, which are then transported to the trunk, limbs, branches, twigs, and leaves. The roots are not typically good for carving because they contain dirt, which dulls carving tools quickly. Also, many roots are twisted, which makes them difficult to carve.

The trunk is the part of the tree without limbs. It connects the roots to the crown and transports food to the roots and food and water throughout the trunk and up to the crown. Because it is less likely to crack or split, wood from the trunk is good wood for carving.

The limbs, branches, twigs, and leaves form the crown of the tree. Leafy branches offer habitats for animals, shade from the sun, protection from the elements, and beauty to the landscape in all four seasons. Food for the tree, called sap, is produced in the leaves through the process of photosynthesis. Limbs, branches, and twigs can all provide good carving wood. Even small twigs can make great material for carving, especially for whittling projects.

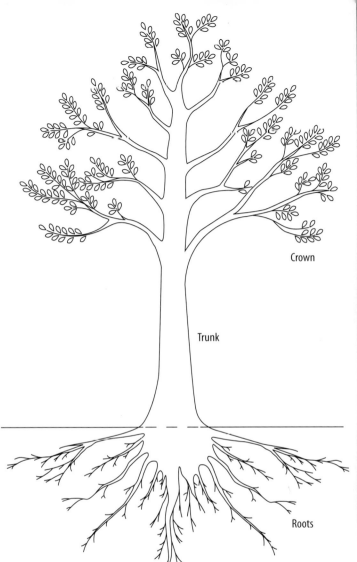

Crown

Trunk

Roots

Do All Trees Have Sap?

Because we use their sap on a regular basis, you may remember certain trees produce sap. Maple trees, for example, produce sap we use to make maple syrup, and birch trees provide the sap used to make birch beer, a fizzy beverage similar to root beer. If you've ever moved or helped plant a pine tree, you've probably ended up with sticky sap on your hands or clothes. Even though we can't always see it, all trees have sap. It's the food made by photosynthesis in the leaves and carried throughout the tree.

All About Wood

Inside the Tree

If we were to cut a tree and look inside, it would look similar to the picture below at right.

The pith, the ring in the very center of the tree, is the beginning of the tree's growth. It is normally softer and darker than the rest of the wood, so try not to use it for carving.

The rings other than the pith are the annual rings. Sometimes they are called growth rings. A tree develops one ring each year, so counting the rings will tell you how old the tree is. The annual rings continue out to the cambium layer.

Each annual ring is made of one band of early wood and one band of late wood. Early wood grows in the spring and is normally light-colored. Late wood grows in the late summer and is normally darker than early wood. Together, the early and late wood help create the beautiful patterns you see in wood, which we call grain.

As a tree grows, eventually the entire trunk is not needed to carry water and food to the leaves. At that point, the tree's center vessels fill with minerals and extractives and become the heartwood of the tree. The heartwood is no longer living but gives added strength to the tree. The minerals and extractives that fill the vessels make the heartwood in some species darker. The area still carrying water and food is known as the sapwood. In some species, such as butternut, cherry, and walnut, you normally carve only the heartwood.

The cambium is the layer between the wood and the bark where the cells divide and the growth of the tree takes place. As cambium cells divide, some become wood and some become bark.

On the outside of the tree is the bark, which is the tree's skin. Bark is made of living and dead cells. The living cells are toward the wood side, and the dead cells are toward the outside of the bark. The bark protects the wood from being damaged by weather, birds, and insects.

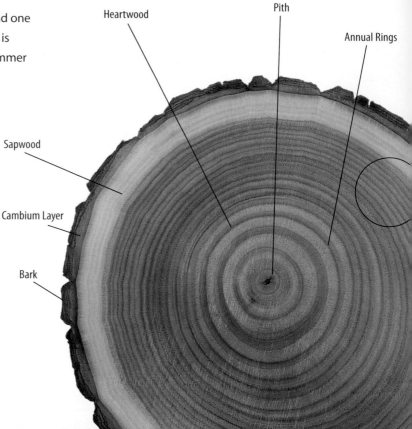

Heartwood

Sapwood

Cambium Layer

Bark

Pith

Annual Rings

How Old Is That Tree?

When a tree is cut down, you can tell how old it is by counting the annual growth rings on the stump. Start at the center, and count to the outside. Wide rings indicate seasons of good growth, while narrow rings suggest seasons of limited growth, perhaps due to bad weather or an insect attack.

Trees are the longest-living organisms on earth. Many trees can live to be 200 years old. The world's tallest trees are the giant redwoods that grow in California, and some are more than 1,000 years old. The oldest trees are gnarly bristlecone pines that grow high in the Rocky Mountains. Some of them are 4,500 years old. Some trees in Australia have root systems that are bigger than an acre.

One of the tallest trees in the world is the General Sherman, a giant redwood in California. The tree measures 275 feet tall and about 25 feet around its trunk.

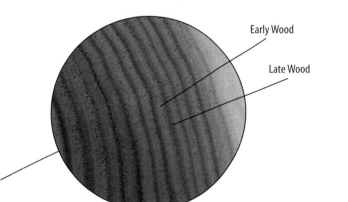

Early Wood

Late Wood

A knot is a kind of defect found inside a tree where a limb broke off the tree. As the tree grew, it covered the spot where the limb was and left a knot. Knots are normally very hard and therefore difficult to carve. When you first start carving, don't carve wood with knots in it.

You may find other defects inside a tree that were caused by things like forest fires and birds and insects breaking through the bark. As the wood grew around the damaged places, those areas, or blemishes, ended up inside the tree. Don't carve wood with a blemish. It takes away from the finished effect of your carving.

Blemish

Knot

All About Wood

Vessels and Grain

If we were to look at a cut section of a tree under a microscope, it would seem as if we were looking into a large bundle of straws. These straws, or vessels, run from the roots to the leaves and carry water and food throughout the tree. The vessel walls are made of fibers that make the walls strong like the walls of a straw.

Understanding the microscopic vessels and the annual rings is important for working with grain. Grain describes the arrangement of vessels in wood. Straight grain, spiral grain, coarse grain, and fine grain all refer to what we see when we look at a piece of wood. The vessels in early wood are larger than those in late wood, and the size differences help make the grain pattern in wood.

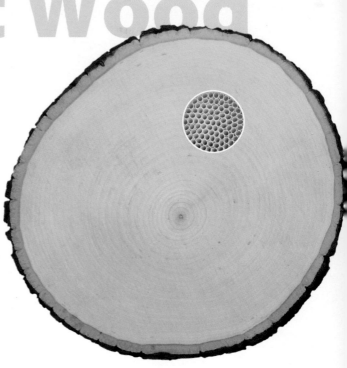

The highlighted area shows how the vessels run up and down the tree trunk.

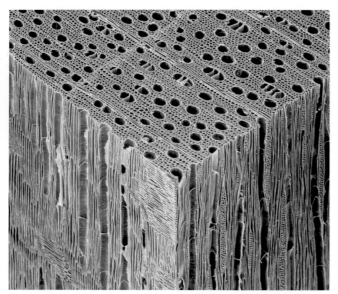

Under a high-powered microscope, the vessels of a tree look like a mass of straws. Photo courtesy N.C. Brown Center for Ultrastructure Studies, SUNY–College of Environmental Science & Forestry, Syracuse, N.Y.

For carvers, grain is most important in describing how you work with wood. It affects every cut you make. For example, if a knife is allowed to go between the vessels, the fibers that make up the vessel walls will tear apart, and the wood will split. This is called "splitting with the grain" and can cause you to lose control of a cut and easily ruin a carving. Make sure every cut you make with your knife or gouge is cutting across the vessels of the wood, not between them. You will learn more about this concept when you practice using your tools in Chapter 3.

Here are some common terms carvers use when working with grain:

Across the grain—Cutting perpendicular to the wood vessels.

With the grain—Cutting parallel to the wood vessels.

Against the grain—Cutting at an angle to the vessels.

Into the grain—Cutting between the vessels.

Splitting with the grain—Tearing of the wood that normally occurs when you cut between the vessels.

This piece of wood is straight-grained, with the grain lines running the length of the board.

When a knife goes between vessels instead of across them, the knife often makes a runaway cut that splits easily and can ruin a carving.

The Best Woods to Carve

There are more than 50,000 different types of trees in the world. You can carve any type of wood, but two of the easier woods to carve are basswood and butternut.

Basswood is one of the most popular woods among carvers because of its fine, even texture. It carves easily, and there is very little difference in color between the heartwood and the sapwood.

Butternut is another good wood to carve. It has about the same texture as basswood, but the heartwood has a beautiful grain pattern and color. Carvers who use butternut don't normally paint the carving. Instead, they apply a clear finish so the grain pattern shows in the finished carving.

Cherry, mahogany, oak, and walnut are also pretty woods, but they are harder to carve. I don't recommend carving one of these woods until you have been carving for a period of time.

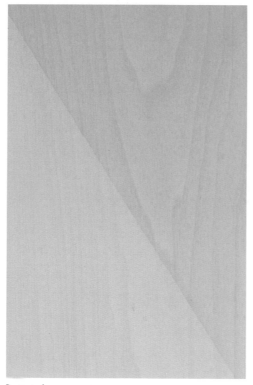

Basswood.

Butternut.

Cypress knees, uniquely shaped wood found in swamps, inspire Alabama carver Carole Jean Boyd. (From *Carving Found Wood* by Vic Hood and Jack A. Williams, 2002, Fox Chapel Publishing, Inc.)

Artist Jim Wright of Tennessee carves in driftwood and says the shape of the wood often suggests what the carving will become. (From *Carving Found Wood* by Vic Hood and Jack A. Williams, 2002, Fox Chapel Publishing, Inc.)

In addition to the woods mentioned on page 8, many people carve found wood. Found wood is any wood in its natural, unaltered state. It can be bark from dead or dying cottonwood trees, cypress knees, knots, weathered wood, or driftwood. Because it is more difficult to carve than boards or other pieces sawn from a tree, I don't recommend found wood for your first project. However, once you have gained some experience, found wood can be an inspiring source of carving wood.

Selecting Wood

Now that you've learned about wood's anatomy and some of the common species for carving, you have the information you need to select a piece of wood for your project. Whatever species you choose, keep an eye out for these things:

Grain. Is the grain straight or twisted? Use straight-grained wood.

Pith. Does the wood have the pith in it? Avoid wood with the pith.

Imperfections. Does the wood have any deformities? Are there any blemishes? Are there any checks, cracks, or knots? Do not use wood with deformities, blemishes, checks, cracks, or knots in the area you want to carve.

Curing. Whatever wood you use, it should be cured, or have had most of the water removed from it. (See "What Is Curing?" in box on bottom right for more information.)

Opt for straight-grained wood because it is easier to carve than wood with twisted grain.

Do not use cracked wood for carving.

What Is Curing?

Curing is the process of removing water from inside wood. Sometimes this process is called seasoning or drying.

When a tree is cut, it contains a huge amount of water. As the water evaporates from the inside, the wood shrinks. When wood shrinks, it often splits. If the wood splits through your carving, it could ruin it.

Air drying is one way to cure wood. In this method, wood is cut and left in the open air until most of the water has evaporated. This can take years. Another way is kiln drying, where the wood is put in a chamber (called a kiln) and the humidity is lowered and the temperature raised. If wood is properly cured, it should not split, which is why you should always carve wood that has been cured.

Where to Get Wood for Carving

One of the best places to get carving wood is from another carver. Try to find a woodcarving club in your area. If you show interest, carvers will be happy to help you get some wood and may even cut out blanks for you.

Woodcarving shows are also a good source. At these shows, there is usually someone selling wood. Carvers attending the shows also may give you wood or blanks if they know you are interested.

Most woodcarving catalogs sell wood, and many of them also sell blanks and roughouts (partially carved blocks).

If you are in a group that does handcrafts, talk to your leaders. They may be able to help you find someone familiar with carving and with the wood and tools you need to get started.

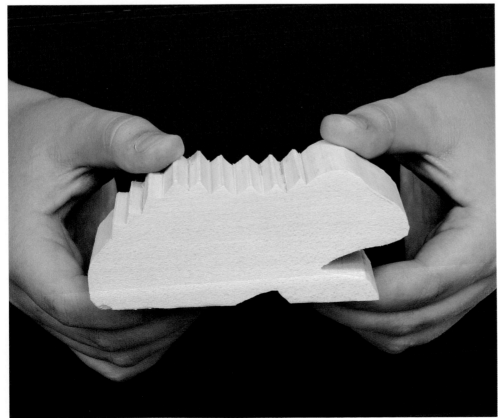

A blank is a block of wood cut to the right size, and it sometimes has the outline of the carving cut out. Cutting the outline before you carve removes much of the waste wood and makes the object easier to carve.

CHAPTER 2

Woodcarving Supplies

In addition to wood and actual carving tools, which we'll discuss in the next chapter, you will want to have some other supplies on hand when carving. This chapter covers the items you'll need and how to use them.

Nonslip Material

Nonslip material—for example, the kind used to line drawers—is excellent for holding wood so it does not slide while you carve it. Nonslip material also helps keep other items in place, such as tools on a workbench. Rolls of it are available at stores that sell household items.

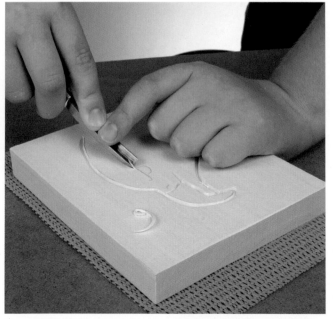

Nonslip material holds the wood in place so it does not slide while you carve it. Simply cut the material slightly larger than your carving block.

Glue

In woodcarving, use yellow wood glue to bond pieces of wood together. It is similar to the white glue you may have used for craft projects, only stronger. Yellow wood glue can be found in most hardware or home improvement stores. (Note: If you do not have yellow wood glue handy, you can use white glue instead.)

Carvers sometimes need glue to make a block large enough for the project they want to create or to join parts together. You will use wood glue for assembling some of the projects in Chapter 4—for example, you will glue the snowman's nose to his body—but you will not need to create bigger blocks for the projects because all of them use readily available wood sizes. If you should ever break off a piece as you're carving,

you can glue the pieces back together by using yellow glue and holding them in place for about 10 minutes.

In the next chapter, you will also use a glue stick to bond sandpaper to particleboard or paint stir sticks to make sharpening tools. Glue sticks are available at most craft stores.

Skills: Gluing Wood Together

Gluing requires more than simply squeezing glue onto the wood. As a first step, make sure that your surfaces are free of sawdust so it won't weaken the bond.

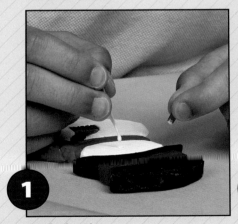

1

Apply the Glue
Spread a small amount on both surfaces you want to bond together. If the area is very small, use a toothpick to apply the glue evenly.

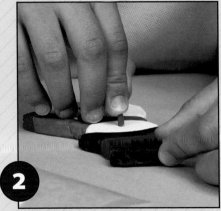

2

Press Together
You can press small pieces together for a minute or two, then leave them alone for an hour so the glue can begin to set. Larger work should be held together overnight with clamps, rubber bands, or tape.

Sandpaper

Sandpaper is covered with abrasive particles that help smooth and shape wood. It can be folded, rolled to shape, or wrapped around objects to help sand hard-to-reach places. Sandpaper is often used to sand a finished carving and to sand between coats of paint or finish. Later on, you will also see how to use sandpaper to sharpen tools. Sandpaper can be found in most hardware or home improvement stores.

Sandpaper has different grits—coarse, medium, fine, and very fine. Each grit has a corresponding number and specific function. (See the chart "Sandpaper Grits" at right.) The size of the grit determines how fast wood is removed. Larger, or coarser, grits remove wood quickly but leave large scratches. You must then use finer and finer grits to remove the scratches. For sanding a carving, you'll need a variety of grits, from about 60 to 220 grit.

Wrap sandpaper around an object, such as a pencil, to help sand the nooks and crannies of a carving.

Sandpaper Grits

Grit	Number	Purpose
Coarse	40 to 60 grit	Fast wood removal
Medium	80 to 120 grit	Smoothing off surface
Fine	150 to 180 grit	Final sanding on wood
Very fine	220 to 240 grit	Creating a very smooth surface

TOUGH · DURABLE U.S.A.
GatorGrit ®
120-C
Garnet Sandpaper
Papier Abrasif Grenat

TOUGH · DURABLE U.S.A.
GatorGrit ®
120-C
Garnet Sandpaper
Papic

Skills: Sanding and Cleaning a Carving

When you have finished a carving, you can leave it so the knife cuts are showing, make the surface slightly smoother but still keep some of the cuts, or sand the surface completely smooth. For a completely smooth surface, start with a medium grit, such as 120, to remove all the facets left from the knife cuts. Then, go to a grit such as 220 to 240 to smooth the surface.

1

Size the Sandpaper
Tear, fold, or otherwise make the sheet easy to hold and maneuver. You can even wrap it around an object to get the right shape. Wrapping it around a flat block makes it easy to sand a flat surface.

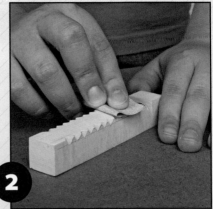

2

Use All of the Grits
Sand through a sequence of sandpaper grits, such as 120 to 180 to 240, to get a smooth surface. When sanding a flat surface, sand in the direction of the wood grain. After sanding with each grit, wipe the surface using a brush or a rag.

Finding Sanding Blocks

Items that you wrap sandpaper around to create sanding blocks don't have to be typical shapes, such as squares, rectangles, or cylinders. They can be odd-shaped items, such as items with curves or other shapes that fit the shape of your carving—so see how many things you can find. Once you have some carving experience under your belt, you can even make your own custom shapes. Just remember, anything you choose needs to stand up to the pressure you'll put on it as you sand, and make sure the part of the item that you hold is safe (free of sharp edges, for example).

3

Clean the Carving
Use a toothbrush to get any sanding dust or chips out of the nooks and crannies of your carving. Then, wipe the surface with a soft cloth to remove the sawdust. Once the sanding and cleaning are complete, the surface is ready for finishing.

Pattern Transfer Supplies

If you want to make your carving look like the project pattern, it is important to accurately transfer the pattern to the wood. These supplies will make transferring a pattern easier.

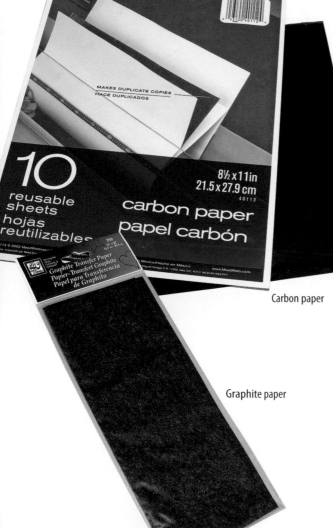

Carbon paper

Graphite paper

Carbon Paper and Graphite Paper

To get an accurate copy of the paper pattern onto the wood, use carbon paper or graphite paper. By placing the pattern on top of the carbon or graphite paper and then taping the pattern to the board, you can trace over the pattern lines to create a copy of the pattern right on the wood. Either product can be purchased at department or office supply stores.

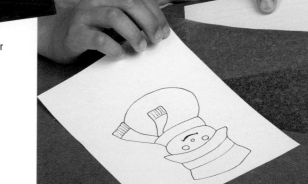

Tracing a pattern onto wood using carbon or graphite paper is easiest for patterns in which you need all of the lines.

Skills: Transferring a Pattern

This method is one of the most effective ways to transfer patterns to wood for carving. It can be used to trace the pattern directly onto the wood or to make a cardboard template.

1

Tape the Pattern
Put a piece of carbon or tracing paper between the pattern and the wood or cardboard. Tape the pattern to the wood or cardboard at the top. Do not tape the bottom.

2

Trace
Using a pencil or a pen, trace over the pattern lines. A colored pencil or pen can be useful for seeing which lines you have traced.

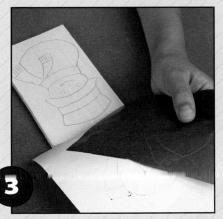

3

Check Your Progress
Because you taped only at the top of the pattern, you can easily check to see if all of the lines have transferred cleanly to the wood or cardboard.

4

Use the Template
If you traced a pattern onto cardboard, cut out the cardboard shape. Then, place the cardboard template onto the wood, and trace around it with a pencil.

Woodcarving Supplies

Cardboard

Instead of tracing the pattern directly onto the wood, you will sometimes want to trace it onto cardboard, especially if the shape is simple. Then, cut out the cardboard pattern, making a template that you can use to make several of the same project. Mark any helpful parts on the template, and trace around the template to apply the pattern to the wood. Cardboard can be purchased at department or office supply stores.

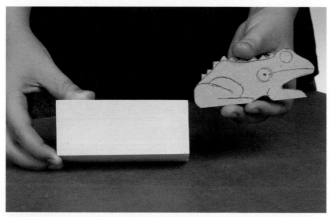

Mark helpful parts, such as drilled holes, on a template. For the frog project in Chapter 4, the position of the drill hole is marked with a pencil hole in the center so it is in exactly the same spot every time you make the project.

Try Making Your Own Patterns

Once you've mastered the skill of tracing patterns very accurately, try changing a pattern. If you are carving a snowman, for example, maybe you will want to change the shape of the hat he is wearing. You might even try creating your own patterns. Pick a favorite drawing or picture and use tracing paper to copy the important parts. However, do not try to capture every detail. It may take a few tries, but the result will be your own unique pattern.

Masking Tape

You are probably familiar with this household tape. For carving, it is useful for taping patterns to wood and sometimes for holding waste wood in place while you work on a fragile part. You can also use masking tape to make a thumb guard, which we will discuss in the next chapter. Masking tape can be purchased at department, hardware, or office supply stores.

Finishing Supplies

There are many different ways to finish, or treat, the wood once you are done carving. You can also leave a carving completely unfinished—without any coat or covering. In this section, we will talk about colored pencils, colored markers, paste wax, paint, and varnish. Whether or not you color your project, you can apply paste wax, clear wax, or varnish (a clear liquid) that coats and protects the surface of your carving and helps keep it from getting dirty. Most of these items can be found at department, hardware, and/or home improvement stores.

Colored Pencils

Though a carving can look great unfinished, it is fun to add color to your work. Colored pencils are a quick, clean way to put color on your carving. I recommend oil pencils, which are similar to colored pencils but use a softer, oil-based pigment. Most oil pencils will allow the wood grain to show through somewhat.

Oil pencils are available in as many as 60 colors, or you can blend them together on a carving to make your own colors. To fix colors so they won't smudge, brush on water-based clear varnish or paste wax. Never brush petroleum-based varnish on the carving, because it will smear the colors.

Colored Markers

Like colored pencils, colored markers are a quick, clean method for adding color to your carving. No special types of markers are needed. You can simply use any markers with the colors you like.

Markers may allow the wood grain to show through, depending on how dark your chosen colors are. Because markers dry quickly and are available in so many different colors, it is better to avoid blending them on the carving. To keep colors from smudging, brush on water-based clear varnish or paste wax. Never brush petroleum-based varnish on the carving, because it will smear the colors.

Thin-tip felt-tip markers of various colors are helpful for doing touch-ups. You can also use them to draw eyes and other details on a carving.

Paste Wax

Paste wax is inexpensive and easy to apply, but it does require more hard work than most other finishes. Though it leaves the wood a natural color the way varnish does, paste wax is not as durable or as protective as varnish. It can be applied over almost any finish or used alone. However, do not apply varnish on top of paste wax; it will ruin the finish.

Commercial paste waxes are generally the same, whatever brand you choose. You can sometimes find paste waxes that have color added, and they will give your carving a little more color, but they won't add as much color as colored pencils, colored markers, or paint.

Skills: Applying Paste Wax

Before you apply any finish, make sure you have sanded the surface well. (See "Sanding and Cleaning a Carving" on page 15.) The more coats of wax you add, the shinier your carving will be. Some carvings look great with shine; other carvings are best left with a low-gloss look.

1

Apply the Wax
Apply paste wax in thin coats using a brush or a rag, and let the carving sit for a few minutes.

2

Buff
Buff off the excess wax with a dry brush and then a soft, lint-free rag. Don't wait too long to remove the excess, or the wax will build up and become difficult to remove. If you do have buildup, apply more wax and it will allow you to easily remove any buildup.

Paint

Acrylic paints are water-based paints that are safe, easy to use, and available at any craft store. When painting, you'll also want to have wax paper to use as a paint palette and some small containers to hold water for cleaning brushes and for thinning paint. Put a covering over your work area so you don't ruin it by getting paint on it. You can use freezer paper, brown wrapping paper, or a section from a cardboard box. Don't use newspaper, because the ink can come off and ruin your carving.

Acrylic paint at full strength will cover the wood completely. If you want the wood grain to show through the paint, thin the paint with water. You can even apply several washes on top of each other—once each has dried—to create different colors, or you can blend the colors together on your paint palette. Because paint colors are easy to change by adding a little more or a little less of one color, experiment with blending colors to find the ones that you like best. Adding a little black or a little white to any color makes a variety of shades.

As with colored pencils and colored markers, brush on water-based clear varnish or paste wax to keep the colors in place. When acrylics are dry, they will not smear.

Watercolor paints can be used the same way acrylic paints are used, except that watercolors are dry and must be mixed with water to dissolve the paints and create the colors.

How Much to Thin Paint

To test if paint is thinned enough for the wood grain to show through it, paint some on a piece of newspaper. If you can see the print through the paint, the paint is thin enough.

Skills: Painting

Make sure you have sanded the surface well before you apply any finish to your project. (See "Sanding and Cleaning a Carving" on page 15.) Then, before you begin the actual painting, prepare all of your materials. Cover your work area, and mix or thin any paint as needed. You can put on gloves if you don't want to get your hands dirty. Take your time painting. A poor paint job can ruin a good carving.

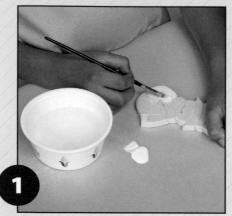

1

Prepare and Apply Paint
Fill a small container half full of water, and set it aside for cleaning your brush. Spread a small bead of paint on wax paper. Apply paint evenly on the surface of the project using a brush.

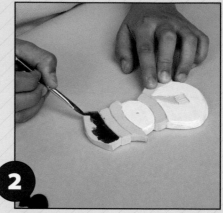

2

Change Colors
Wash the brush before changing colors. Then, continue painting your project.

Varnish

Especially if your carving is going to be handled, you will want to apply varnish to protect it from fingerprints and dirt. Varnish is available as water based or petroleum based. Water-based varnish is easier to clean up and is not toxic like petroleum-based varnish.

Skills: Varnishing

Make sure you have sanded the surface well before you apply any finish to your project. (See "Sanding and Cleaning a Carving" on page 15.) Before you begin varnishing, gather all of your materials. Wear gloves when you are using varnish.

1

Apply the Varnish
Dip the tip of your brush in the container of varnish and brush a thin coat onto the project. You don't want any puddles or pools of varnish on the carving. Use a lint-free rag to wipe off any puddles that form. In the photo, we are using a disposable foam brush.

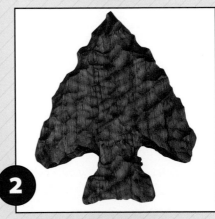

2

Add More Coats
Set the carving aside, and allow it to dry. You can simply put it on a piece of wax paper or scrap wood for easy cleanup. You could also pound three nails the whole way through a piece of scrap wood, and then rest the carving on the nail points so air can easily dry the whole piece. Once the varnish is completely dry, apply another coat. Apply a total of two to three coats using this method.

CHAPTER 3
Tools

Many types of tools are used when carving wood. I'll show you some of the tools and how to use them. But you don't need all of the tools to get started. All you need is one sharp knife and a piece of wood. After you have tried carving and if you know you want to continue, you may then want to buy some of these different tools.

Safety Tools

If you're going to hold a piece of wood in your hand as you carve it with a knife, wear a safety glove and a thumb guard. Clamps, discussed later in this chapter on page 31, are also safety tools because they keep your hands away from cutting edges. For the exercises and projects in this book, you will always clamp the wood when carving with a gouge or a V-tool.

Even if you are wearing safety items, you should be extra careful at all times. Carving tools are sharp and can cut you if you don't use them properly. Also, be sure to keep a first-aid kit handy when you are carving.

Kevlar gloves.

Safety Glove

A safety glove helps protect you from being cut by your knife. You wear it on the hand holding the wood.

Some gloves are made of Kevlar, the same material from which bulletproof vests are made. An even safer glove is a stainless steel one, the kind used by people who handle sheets of metal or glass. This type of glove has a fine steel wire through the middle of each thread. It will give you the most protection as you carve. Both types of gloves are available from woodcarving stores or woodcarving catalogs and come in a variety of sizes.

Be aware at all times that a safety glove will protect you from some slashing cuts but will not give you much protection from a stab cut.

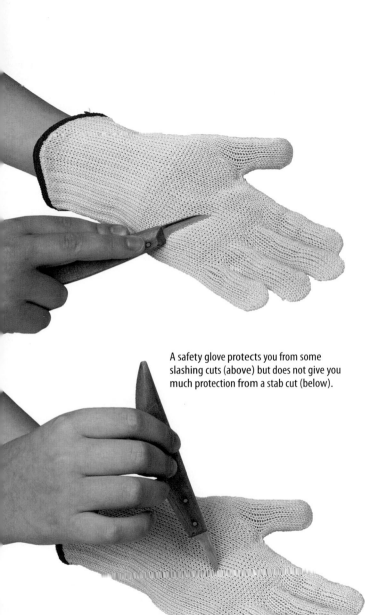

A safety glove protects you from some slashing cuts (above) but does not give you much protection from a stab cut (below).

Stainless steel glove.

Measuring Glove Size

To determine what size glove you should wear, measure around the knuckles of your hand as shown at right, and then use this chart to find the proper size glove for the best fit.

Glove Size	Measurement around Hand in Inches
Glove Sizes	
Extra small	6½ to 7½
Small	7½ to 8½
Medium	8½ to 9½
Large	9½ to 10½
Extra large	10½ to 11½

Measure here

Thumb Guard

A thumb guard is made of leather with an elastic band and is placed on the thumb of the hand holding the knife. The elastic band keeps the guard on your thumb. These guards come in different sizes, so buy one that fits snugly.

You can also make a thumb guard using a self-adhering bandage materials called vet wrap or by using masking tape or duct tape. Vet wrap is available at stores that carry horse supplies or from carving catalogs. Some catalogs call it finger wrap or wimp wrap. Vet wrap sticks to itself, but not to your skin.

First-Aid Kit

Having a first-aid kit available just in case of an accident is a good idea. Keep it in your work area. If you do not already have these items in the house, buy a kit or put a kit together with at least some bandages, sterile wipes, gauze, a pair of tweezers, and a magnifying glass.

Make Your Own Thumb Guard

It is easy to make your own thumb guard. Plus, if you get cuts in the tape, masking tape, or duct tape, you can simply add more layers. When the thumb guard gets too thick, make a new one. Here's how to make a thumb guard.

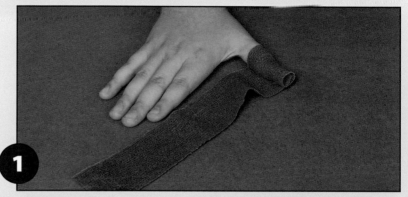

Cut the roll of self-adhering tape in half so that you end up with two separate rolls, equally sized. Then, cut a piece about 12" long, and wrap it around your thumb past the knuckle. If you use masking tape or duct tape, use tape that is about 1" wide and wrap the first layer with the sticky side out, and then wrap about six more layers with the sticky side down over the first layer

Continue to wrap the tape around your thumb, shaping it to your thumb as you go.

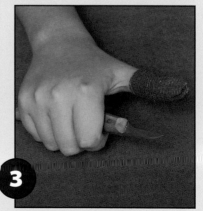

Make sure the fit is snug, and you are ready to carve.

Caring for Your tools

Because you will have spent money purchasing your tools and time sharpening them, you will want to keep them as nice as possible. Here are some tips for caring for your tools:

Protect the cutting edges. When you are not using your tools, put something over the cutting edges to protect them. Remember to be careful when putting protectors on the blades or putting your tools away.

Keep your tools dry and in a safe place. Doing so will prevent the tools from rusting and minimize the potential of someone getting cut. An old shoebox works great to hold your tools.

Keep your tools away from hard objects. When using your tools, never place them where another tool or hard object can hit the cutting edges. If something hard hits the sharp edge of a tool, it can nick the blade. A nicked blade leaves little lines in the wood as you carve. If a tool gets a nick, you will need to remove it by sharpening the tool.

Keep your work area clean. Cleaning your work area regularly helps protect your tools from dust and spills, which can dull your blades or cause rust.

Plastic tubing also makes good blade protectors. You can buy different sizes of tubing at any hardware store for just pennies per foot.

Sinking tools into pieces of dense insulation protects the cutting edges.

Measuring and Marking Tools

Measuring and marking wood accurately is important for patterns that are measured or must be fit to the wood and for project parts to fit together properly. Rulers and squares lay out dimensions, and pencils draw marks and lines.

Ruler

A ruler is made of wood, metal, or plastic, and has markings to measure distances between two points. You will use a ruler often as you carve. A 6" ruler is a good one to have on hand.

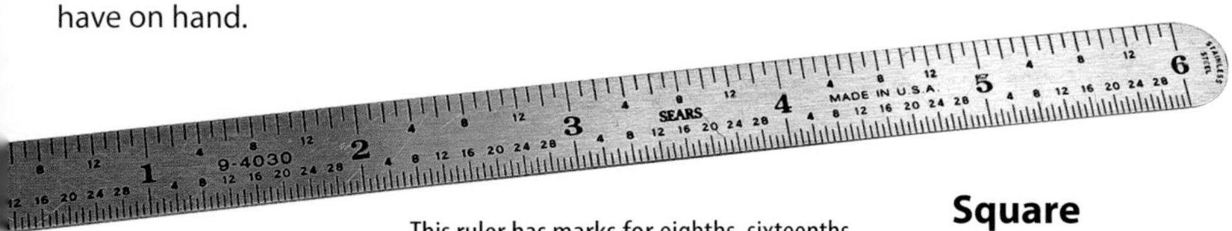

This ruler has marks for eighths, sixteenths, and thirty-seconds of an inch.

Square

A square's primary purpose is to measure right (90°) angles. Many squares also measure 45° angles. Some also can measure the center of a dowel and angles other than 45° and 90°.

The particular square shown below is called a combination square. All combination squares have at least two parts: a rule and a head. In Chapter 4, you'll be using a square to lay out letters to be carved on a name plaque, to ensure they are straight and square (at 90°) to one another.

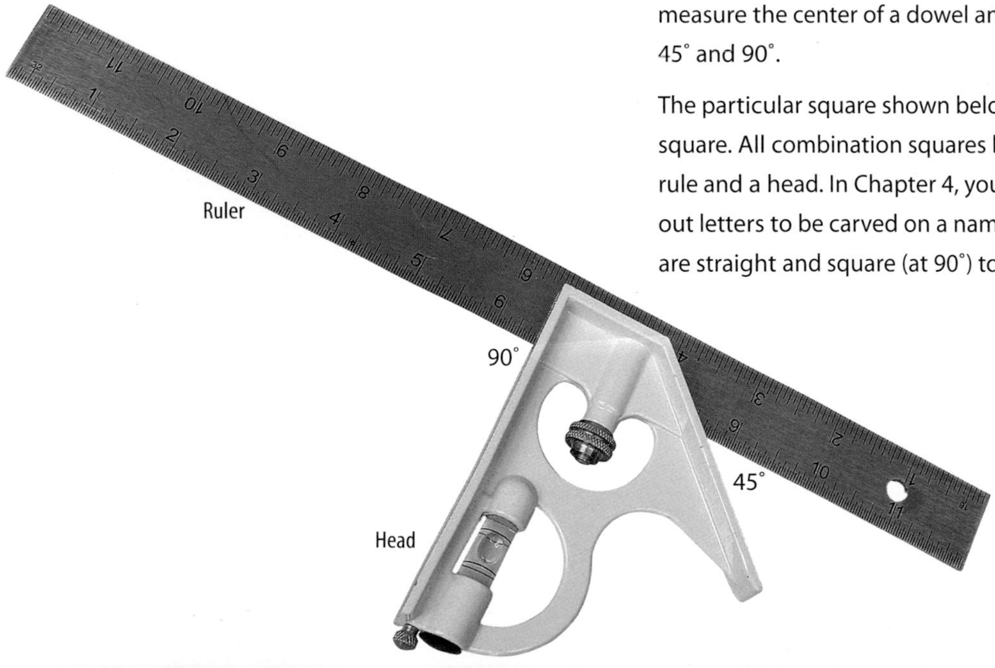

Ruler

90°

45°

Head

Tools

Pencil

Using a regular pencil is the best and easiest way to mark measurements and draw lines on your carving blocks. Remember to keep the pencil sharpened so your lines are crisp and clear.

Skills: Measuring and Marking

Freehand drawing is another common method of pattern transfer. This technique allows you to modify sections as you go, if needed, using the pattern as a guide. Rulers, squares, and other measuring devices are often used in freehand drawing. Measurement marks and reference lines are sometimes more helpful than drawing the complete pattern on the wood. In this practice exercise, you will use a square, but you can use the same technique with a ruler.

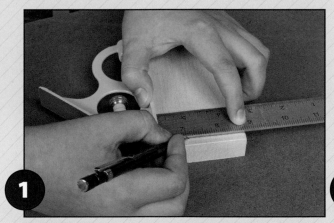

1

Measure
Make two marks, each ¼" from one side of the board. Also measure and make two marks ¼" from the top of the board. Do the same for the bottom of the board.

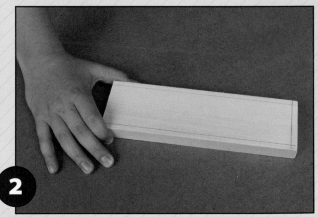

2

Mark
Hold the fence of the square tight against the edge of the wood with one hand, slide it up to one pair of marks, and then draw the pencil along the edge of the square to connect the dots. Do this for each set of marks. When you are finished, you should have a line on each of the three sides.

Clamping Tools

Whenever you can, you should clamp your carving so both hands can be on the tool as you carve. While a glove and a thumb quard help protect your hands, clamps make carving even safer. Having both hands on the tool helps keep them away from the cutting edge of the blade. For the exercises and projects in this book, you will always clamp the carving when working with gouges and V-tools. Clamps, vises, and a carving table are all useful for holding a carving in place.

There are a variety of clamps available. Pick the type that works best for you.

Clamps

Clamps hold an object in place or hold objects to each other, often to glue them together. There are many different types of clamps, but most clamps for woodworking have sliding jaws so they can be tightened onto different size projects. If you use a metal clamp to hold the object as you carve, place pieces of wood between the jaws of the clamp and the piece you're carving so if the tool ever slips, it hits wood rather than metal.

Skills: Clamping

A quick-set clamp with a sliding jaw is easy to use once you know the trick: Hold the fixed jaw in position with one hand while you bring the movable jaw up to it.

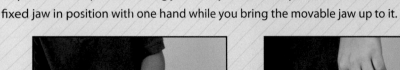

1

Open the Clamp
Turn the screw handle so the round clamp pad is close to the jaw. This provides room for adjusting the clamp.

2

Plant the Fixed Jaw
Hold the fixed jaw of the clamp steady and flat against the work.

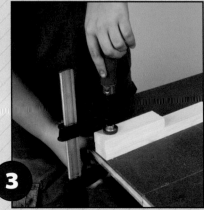

3

Set the Clamp
Slide the movable jaw along the clamp bar until the pad rests flat on the wood. Tighten the clamp handle.

Tools

Vise

Vises are also a good way to hold your project as you carve. They come in a variety of designs, but some are easier to use than others. If you buy a vise, it should firmly hold the piece you're going to carve, let you place the carving where you want it quickly and easily, and not be so large it gets in the way as you carve.

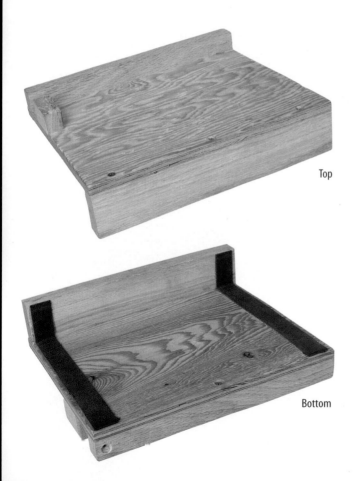

Top

Bottom

Carving Table

A carving table holds a project as you carve. The stops along the back and on the side help keep the object from moving. If you are right handed, the short stop should be on the left side; if you are left handed, it is on the right. Leave a small gap between the backstop and the short stop so you can easily remove any chips that collect in this area. A good work surface is about 9" deep by 12" wide.

Use the plans at right to build your own carving table. Attach some nonslip material on the bottom to protect the surface on which you place the carving table and to keep the carving table from moving as you carve. You also can put a towel under the carving table to protect the surface beneath it.

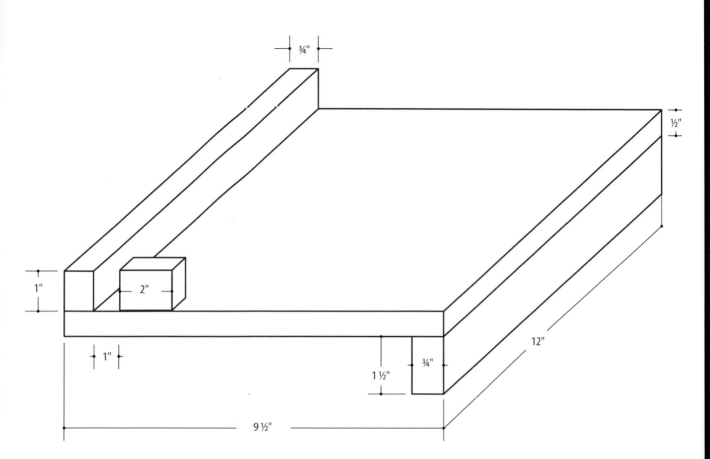

Use these plans to build your own carving table. You will need to employ your measuring and marking skills (page 30), your clamping skills (page 31), and your sawing skills (page 36).

Saws

For the projects in this book, you will be cutting wood with handsaws. You will not actually carve with a handsaw, but these tools can quickly remove excess wood from the blank so you can get to the carving part faster. There are a variety of handsaws available. You will be using a coping saw for finer, curved cuts and a backsaw for straight cuts and stop cuts. Whatever type of saw you are using, never put your fingers in harm's way.

Coping Saw

This type of saw has a very thin blade stretched between the ends of a U-shaped frame. A threaded bolt connects the frame and the blade to the handle. A coping saw excels at detailed work because its thin blade can cut tight radiuses.

The blade can be quickly changed by loosening the handle and removing the blade from its holders. When replacing a blade, the teeth should face toward the handle because the saw cuts when it is pulled toward you. You can cut a piece from the center of your project by loosening the blade and feeding it through a drilled hole.

Skills: Making Curved Cuts

When using a coping saw, don't press too hard on the thin blade, or it will not cut straight. Practice using a coping saw before you attempt to cut out your project.

1

Start the Saw
Draw the layout line, and clamp the wood upright in a vise. Holding the coping saw in both hands, start to saw by making short, light cuts.

2

Follow the Layout Line
Once the blade is into the wood, use the full length of the blade as you steer the saw along your layout line. Remember, the saw cuts on the pull stroke.

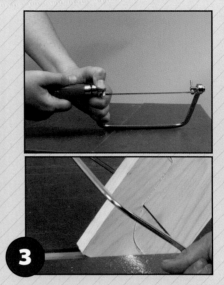

3

Turn the Saw Frame
If the saw frame bangs into the wood, loosen the handle, and turn the blade so it clears. Then, tighten the handle. Keep the blade holders in line with each other.

Backsaw

A backsaw has a thin blade and a stiff back. The stiff back gives the blade strength so it won't bend easily. This is a useful saw to cut straight lines or to make stop cuts. Backsaws come in different sizes. Use larger saws to cut off larger pieces of wood.

Skills: Making Basic Saw Cuts

Before you saw, draw layout lines using the technique described in "Measuring and Marking" on page 30. Draw the first line ½" from the end of the piece. Draw another line ⅜" from the first line. Turn the piece on its side, and extend the first line ⅜" down the side. Draw another line from the second line down to meet the extension of the first line.

You can saw with the wood in a vise or with the wood clamped flat on the table. Try both ways to learn what is more comfortable for you. Make sure that the work can't move around and that the sawing line extends beyond the bench so you don't accidentally saw into the bench. You don't have to press hard with the saw to make it work.

1

Start the Saw
Stand with your sawing arm in line with the cut. Brace your other hand on the wood. Make short, light strokes to break the corner and get the teeth into the wood. Keep the saw square to the wood. Make longer strokes to extend the cut all the way along the line.

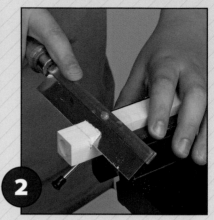

2

Saw the Line
Tilt the backsaw, and follow the second line to remove the piece of wood. Slow down as you reach the end of the cut, and again make short, light strokes. The piece should easily come free.

Eggbeater Drill with Bits

Drills are used to remove wood in selected areas, to make holes for inserting screws or for inserting other pieces of the carving, or to make holes in general.

The eggbeater drill can make holes up to ¼" in diameter. A chuck, or a sleeve you turn to open and close the jaws inside, holds the drill bit. In this book, you'll use a ⅛" twist drill bit, a ½" brad point bit, and a ⅝" spade bit.

Eggbeater drill with twist drill bits.

⅝" spade bit.

You need both hands to work the drill, so always clamp the workpiece to the bench or trap it in a vise. Clamp it onto a piece of scrap wood; otherwise, the drill might tear the wood as it chews out through the back. To work the drill, press and guide the handle with one hand, while turning the crank with the other hand.

Skills: Drilling Holes

Let's practice making holes with the drill and bit. To begin, usually you will clamp the wood to be drilled so it can't slide as you work. Because our piece was small and easier to see without the clamp, we used nonslip material to hold the piece in place, but you will probably want to clamp it down. Also, because we were not drilling the whole way through the wood, we did not put a piece of scrap wood underneath, but you may want to include a scrap piece just in case.

1

Mark the Drill Hole
Measure and mark the drill hole. In this case, the hole is part of the pattern for the snowman (his nose). Choose a drill bit the exact size of the hole you want. Put the bit all the way into the chuck, and tighten it as hard as you can.

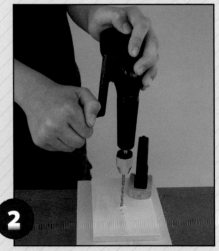

2

Drill the Hole
Make sure the drill is aligned with the hole you drew. Then, turn the drill crank to make the drill bite into the wood. It will start to cut and lift the chips of wood out of the hole.

Tools

Knives

A carving knife is one of the first tools most carvers purchase. Carving knives come in all shapes and sizes. Some of the most common choices are a craft knife, a pocketknife, and a fixed-blade knife. Most carvers use a fixed-blade knife, but all of these knives perform the same tasks and make the same cuts. In the projects in this book, we show all three in use. If you can, experiment with all of them to see which knife works best for you. Let's talk a little bit about each.

Where Do You Get Tools?

Carving tools are available from any carving store or from woodcarving catalogs. Another good source is woodcarving shows. There will usually be at least one business selling carving tools at the show.

You can buy individual carving tools or get them as a set of tools. I recommend starting with a straight-blade carving knife with a blade no longer than 1½".

If you want to get a gouge, a good size to start with is a #9 ⅜". A good size V-tool is ⅜".

If you are going to do small carvings and you want to buy a set of tools, a popular set is one such as this.

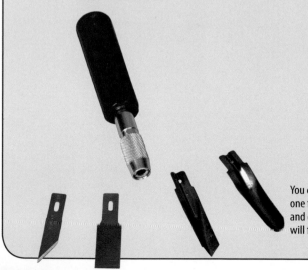

You can also get a set such as this one from X-Acto. It has one handle and different types of blades that will fit into the handle.

Craft Knife

A craft knife set has various shaped blades that all fit into one handle and can be easily replaced. The handle has a knurled collar that holds the blade in place. Be sure to tighten the knurled collar so the blade will not fall out. Always be careful when removing or inserting the blades. The blades are very sharp and can quickly cut you.

A craft knife and blade set do not cost very much, so it is an inexpensive way to get started carving.

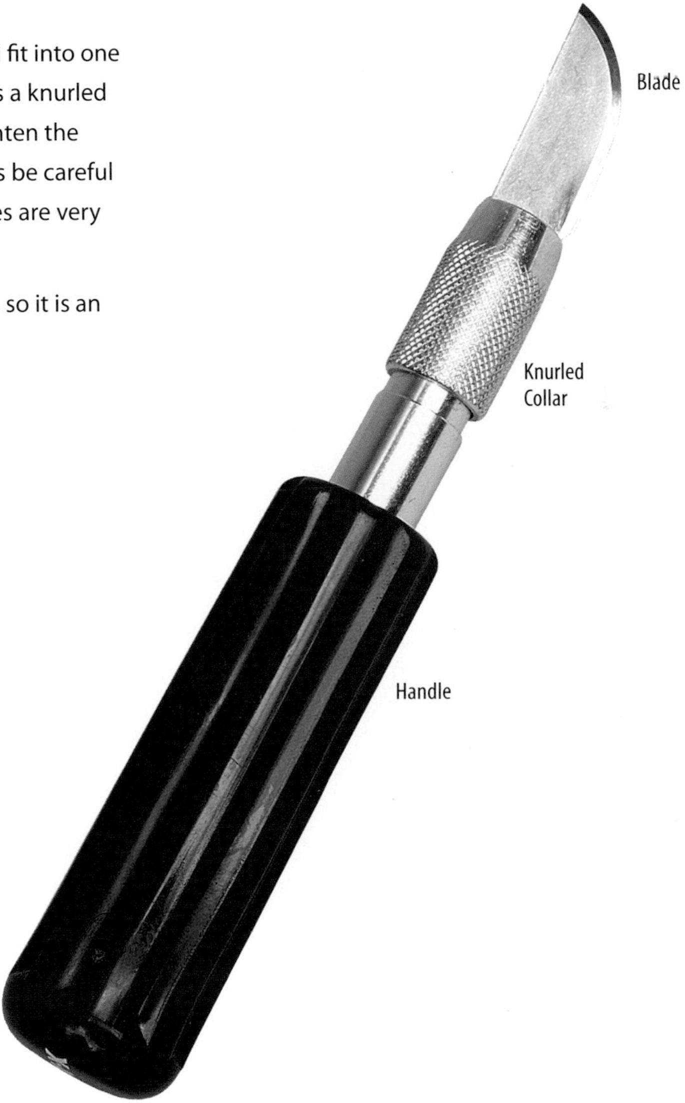

Blade

Knurled Collar

Handle

Craft knives like these might fit your hand best.

Tools

Pocketknife

Pocketknives have one or more blades that fold into the handle so the knife can be safely carried in your pocket. Regardless of how many blades they have, all pocketknives have the same parts.

If you use a pocketknife for carving, use a knife with no more than three blades. There are other knives that contain many blades and even some tools, but these knives become large and hard to hold for carving.

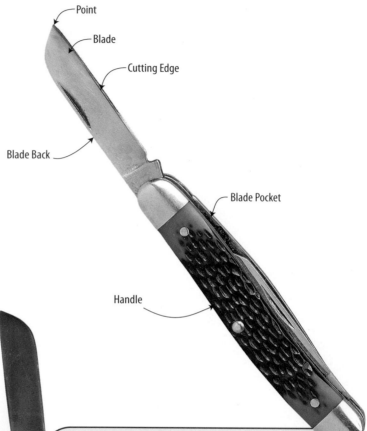

Point
Blade
Cutting Edge
Blade Back
Blade Pocket
Handle

Rules for Pocketknife Safety

Always keep your pocketknife closed and in your pocket when not using it.

- Never carry around an open knife.

- Never throw your knife.

- Always close your knife before you pass it to someone else.

- Don't pry with it.

- Never take your knife to school.

- Keep your knife clean and dry.

How to Safely Open and Close a Pocketknife

Have an adult present the first few times you practice doing this.

To open the knife if you are right-handed:

1

Hold the knife in your left hand, and put your right-hand thumb in the nail slot.

2

Pull the blade out with your right hand.

3

Continue to pull the blade until it snaps open.

To close the knife if you are right-handed:

1

Hold the knife in your right hand, keeping your fingers away from the blade. Place your left-hand fingers behind the blade.

2

Carefully push the blade forward, keeping your fingers behind the blade.

3

Continue pushing the blade until it snaps closed.

Tools

Fixed-Blade Knife

A fixed-blade knife has the blade permanently set in the handle. Most experienced carvers use this type of knife. If you buy a fixed-blade knife, get one with a straight blade no longer than 1½". This type of knife is easy to handle and easy to sharpen. If properly used, it will stay sharp for a long time before it will need to be sharpened again.

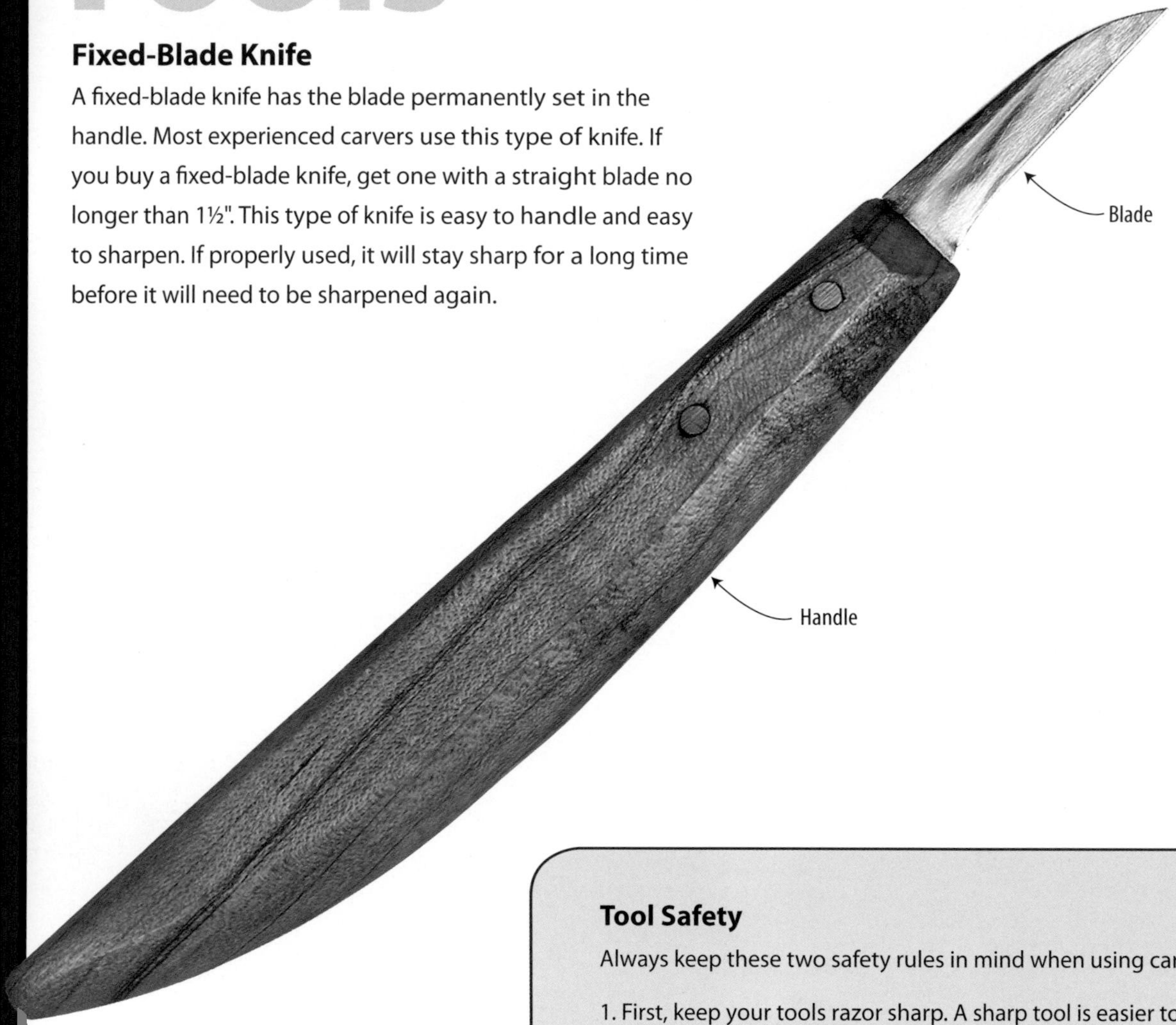

Blade

Handle

Tool Safety

Always keep these two safety rules in mind when using carving tools:

1. First, keep your tools razor sharp. A sharp tool is easier to control as it slices through the wood than a dull one.

2. Keep focused at all times, and make sure you know where your body parts are in relation to the tool blade. Never put anything that can bleed in front of the blade.

Skills:
Making Knife Cuts

This section covers all of the cuts you can make with any of the knives described on pages 38 to 42, even though the fixed-blade knife is shown in the photos.

Keep in mind that whenever you are carving, you should not be using your arms to make the cuts. All of the cuts are intended to be made using the muscles of your hand. Also, make sure that the hand holding the knife is always in contact with the wood.

We'll start with the pull cut and the push cut because they are the ones you will use most often. Each exercise will also show you how to hold the knife to perform that specific cut.

Before you begin, make sure you have an adult with you at all times when you're working with carving tools.

Get ready to carve by gathering your materials. You'll need a thin piece of basswood, your knife of choice, a carving glove, and a thumb guard. Put on your carving glove and thumb guard before you start to carve. Remember, even when you wear protective items, never put your hands or fingers in a location where they can get cut.

Basswood

Knife

Carving glove

Thumb guard

Skills: Pull Cut

The pull cut is the one used most often as you carve. It is also called a paring cut because you hold the knife as you do when you pare (peel) an apple or a potato.

Make small cuts when you begin so that you have more control. Continue to practice this exercise until you feel comfortable doing the pull cut.

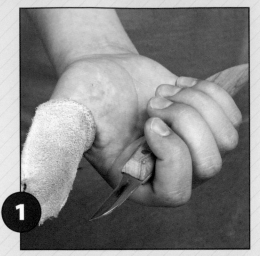

Hold the Knife
Lay the knife in your hand with the cutting edge of the blade facing toward your thumb. Then, wrap your fingers around the handle.

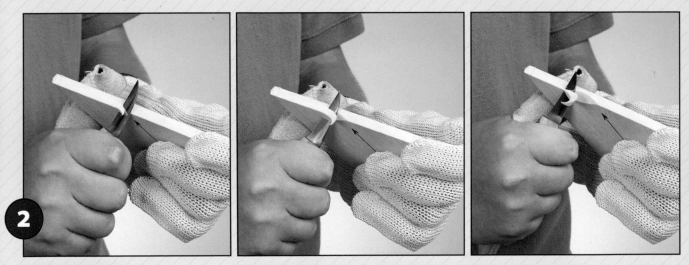

Pull the Knife
Turn the knife over, and place your thumb in a safe location on the wood, near where you want the blade to exit the wood. Pull the knife through the wood using your hand muscles by curling your fingers in the direction you want to pull the knife through the wood.

Skills: Push Cut

Take the time to learn how to make this cut. There will be many areas in a carving where this cut works better than the pull cut. Keep practicing the push cut until you feel comfortable doing it.

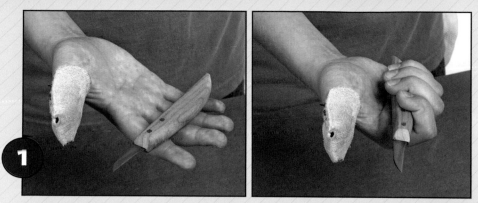

1

Hold the Knife
Hold the knife with the cutting edge of the blade facing away from you. Then, close your hand over the knife handle, and rotate your hand so the palm of your hand is facing down.

2

Position Your Thumbs
Place your right thumb on the back of the blade. Place your left thumb on the back of the blade, touching your right thumb.

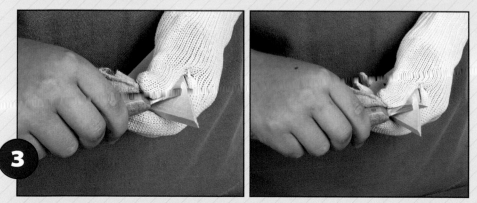

3

Push the Blade
Push the blade through the wood with your thumbs.

Don't Let the Knife Go Between Vessels

When you're carving, always cut so that the knife is never given an opportunity to go between the vessels (the grain) in the wood. To show you why, I've cut this piece at an angle across the grain of the wood.

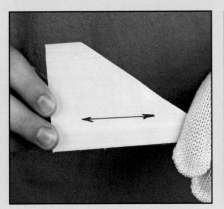

The line shows the direction of the grain.

If I cut so the blade of my carving tool goes between the grain, the wood will split, and I will lose control of my cut.

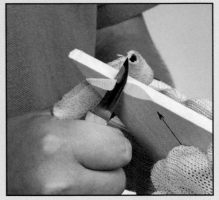

If I cut across the grain, I will always have control of the cut and get a smooth cut surface.

Learning how to do pull cuts and push cuts proficiently will save you time and help eliminate splitting. The piece of wood below has been cut to show how you can cut from each direction and get clean cuts without turning the piece around. (The grain runs in the direction of the arrow.)

Use a pull cut to cut toward the bottom of the piece. When your knife reaches the bottom, it will attempt to go between the grain.

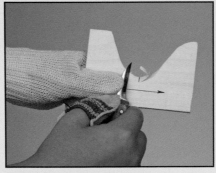

Do a push cut from the other side.

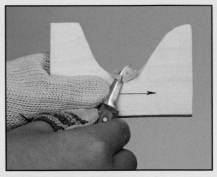

When you reach the bottom of the piece, the wood will fall out, and you will have smooth cuts in both directions to the bottom.

Skills: Stop Cut

The stop cut is used to separate a section of wood you want to remove from a section you want to keep. Because the stop cut is perpendicular to the other cuts you're making, you can make cuts toward it without cutting into wood you don't want to remove.

Any tool that cuts wood can make a stop cut. The tools most often used are a knife, a V-tool, or a saw. If you use your knife, hold it as you do when you draw a line with a pencil. To help make a stop cut with your knife, you can place your left-hand fingers on the back of the blade.

1

Start the Cut
Hold the knife like a pencil, with the blade perpendicular to the wood, and slice straight through the wood. If you want a deep stop cut, do not try to do it in one cut; instead, make several cuts in the same line.

2

Cut to the Full Depth
You can now remove wood up to the stop cut without disturbing the wood you want to save. Tilt the blade and remove the waste wood up to the stop cut. You also do not need a thumb guard when chip cutting. The only time you need a glove and a thumb guard is when you hold the piece you are carving in your hand as you carve.

Skills: Incised Cut

The best way to learn how to make this cut is to draw a lazy S on a board. (Your objective is to remove the S and have the pencil line down the middle of the piece you removed.) For incised cuts, hold your knife as you would to make a stop cut.

1

Cut the First Side
Place your knife about 1/16" from one side of the S, and tilt it about 45° away from the line. Pull your knife through the wood, keeping the same distance away from the line as you cut along this side.

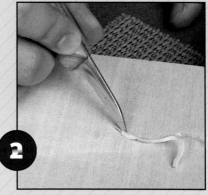

2

Cut the Second Side
Place your knife on the other side of the S at the same distance away, and again tilt the knife about 45° away from this side of the line. Pull your knife through the wood, and remove the S. Is it down the middle of the piece? Practice until you can do this with ease.

Skills: Score Cut

This cut is similar to a stop cut, but it is normally done at a spot where you want to make a line in the wood or where you want to break a piece of wood.

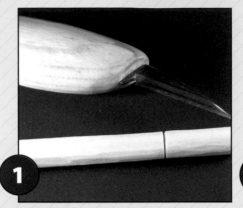

1

Cut the Line
Hold the knife as you would to make a stop cut, and cut a line part of the way through the wood.

2

Break the Wood
Break the wood at the score cut.

Skills: Chip Cut

A chip cut is a set of three cuts that removes a triangular chip. You will use this cut to create decorative designs on some of the projects in this book.

Start by measuring and marking two straight lines that are ¼" apart and about 3" long on a piece of scrap wood. Make small marks every ¼" along the top line. Mark every ¼" along the bottom line, starting the first mark ⅛" over from the first mark on the top line. Then, draw a series of triangles using the marks.

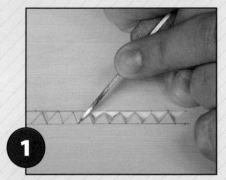

1

Cut the First Side
Tilt your knife about 45°, and hold the knife as shown, with your thumb on the wood. Cut the first side of one triangle down to the bottom line.

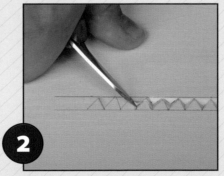

2

Cut the Second Side
Tilt your knife 45° the other way, and position your hand as shown. Cut along the second side.

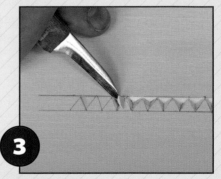

3

Cut the Bottom
Tilt the knife again, and cut along the bottom of the triangle and remove the chip.

Gouge

A gouge is a tool that has a curved, trough-like blade. The curve of the blade is known as the sweep of the gouge. The sweep of a gouge is labeled by number, and the numbers go from #3 to #9. The bigger the number, the more the blade curves. Gouges with bigger curves can cut deeper in one stroke than gouges with small curves.

Gouges are very useful tools for carving. Both knives and gouges can perform many of the same cuts. However, there are three basic cuts you make with a gouge: the concave cut, where you cut a channel in the wood; the convex cut, where you turn the tool over to round a surface; and the plunge cut, where you drive the tool into the wood as you do with a stop cut. You will only be using the concave and plunge cuts for the projects in this book. To keep control of a gouge, never let its wings (the points of the blade) go under the wood's surface.

The Parts of a Gouge

Gouges and V-tools have the following parts:

Handle—Normally made of a hard wood; can be round, hexagon, or oblong and various lengths.

Ferrule—A metal ring, or insert, that adds strength to the handle.

Tang—The part of the blade that connects the tool to the handle; is inserted into a hole drilled in the handle.

Blade—The body of the tool.

Outside bevel—The angle that forms the cutting edge; the area between the toe and the heel.

Toe—The front of the cutting edge.

Heel—The back of the cutting surface.

Inside bevel—The small angle on the inside of the cutting edge; gives strength to the cutting edge.

Wings—The outside edges of the blade; the width of a tool is measured from wing to wing.

Shoulder—The flared section of the blade at the bottom of the tang; prevents the blade from pushing into the handle.

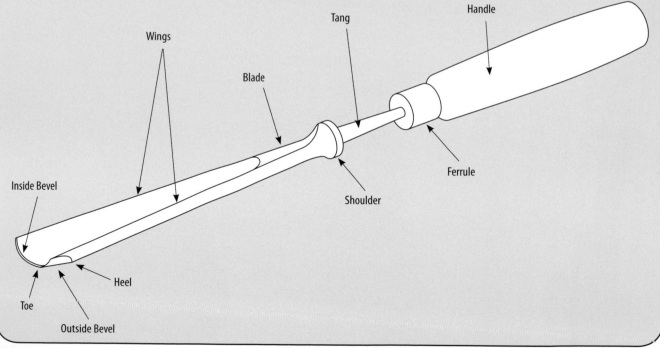

Skills: Gouge Cut

The method shown here is a general method for removing wood. You can also use the same technique with a V-tool. Before you begin, place a piece of wood in a clamp or a vise or on a carving table.

1

Push the Tool
Push the tool into the wood.

2

Continue the Cut
As you continue to push forward, lower the handle toward the wood surface, and the tool will come out of the wood.

3

Never Pry
Never push the tool into the wood and pry the wood out. If you pry, you will tear the vessels and not get a smooth cut. Prying can also break the cutting edge of the tool.

Holding a Gouge

For any of the exercises or projects in this book, never hold the wood in your hand when you carve with a gouge or a V-tool. Always clamp the wood with a vise or a clamp, use a carving table, or plant the wood on non-slip material as shown here.

When the wood is stationary, place the handle of the tool in the palm of your right hand. To give added control, place the first two fingers of your left hand on top of the shank, and place your thumb under the shank. The pad of your left hand, or your first two fingers of your left hand, should always be placed on the item as you carve it.

Skills: Removing Wood to a Stop Cut

The method shown here is a general method for removing wood. You can also use the same technique with a V-tool. Before you begin, place a piece of wood in a clamp or a vise or on a carving table.

Make the Stop Cut
Use your knife to make a stop cut, as described in "Stop Cut" on page 47.

Push the Gouge
Hold your gouge in your right hand, as described on page 51, and place the cutting edge about 1" from the stop cut. Push the gouge into the wood, and remove the piece up to the stop cut.

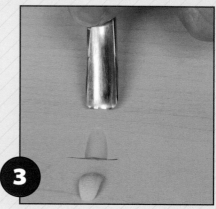

Remove the Chip
The piece should fall out.

Skills: Making a Plunge Cut

Use the plunge cut to make gouge-shaped impressions in the wood. Hold the gouge as you normally do.

Press the Gouge into the Wood
Rest the gouge on the wood, and then, push it in. You can gently wiggle it to help press it in. Turn the gouge or use several passes to make a complete circle.

V-Tool

Also called a parting tool, a V-tool has a V-shaped cutting edge. This tool is used to outline a carving and to make decorative cuts. A V-tool has the same parts as a gouge.

Instead of being labeled by number as gouges are, V-tools are listed by degree of the cutting angle. They are available with angles of 30°, 35°, 45°, 55°, 60°, 75°, 90°, 100°, or 120°. A 60° cutting angle is the most popular.

Skills: Removing Wood with a V-Tool

Using a V-tool is very similar to using a gouge. You hold both tools the same way. (See "Holding a Gouge" on page 51.)

For this exercise, start by placing a piece of wood in a clamp or a vise or on your carving table. Draw a lazy S line on the board.

1

Push the V-tool
Remove the lazy S with your V-tool. Keep the pencil line in the center of the piece you're removing.

2

Practice
Continue carving with this same technique. When you can keep the line in the center of the piece you've removed, you have control of your V-tool.

Tools

Sharpening Tools

In this section, we'll look at common sharpening tools, including sharpening stones, sandpaper, honing compound, strops, and India taper triangles. We'll also go over the basics of sharpening your carving tools. You must have sharp tools to carve wood. Dull tools are more dangerous than sharp tools. A sharp tool cuts the wood easily, so you can concentrate on the cut you're making. Use a dull tool, and you'll need to concentrate on how much pressure you need to drive the tool through the wood. If the tool slips, you could easily cut yourself.

A sharp tool will leave a shiny surface where you cut. A dull tool will tear the wood, leaving a rough surface where you cut.

For More on Sharpening

There are a number of books on sharpening that will teach you how to sharpen carving tools. Another good source is my DVD *Sharpening Simplified*.

SHARPENING SIMPLIFIED

A SIMPLE, PROVEN METHOD TO SHARPEN YOUR CARVING KNIVES, CHISELS, GOUGES, "V" TOOLS AND MICRO TOOLS.

DVD

Everett Ellenwood

Sandpaper and a homemade sandpaper sharpening tool.

Sharpening Stones and Sandpaper

There are many types of sharpening stones available to shape and sharpen your tools. The most common are water stones, oilstones, diamond stones, and Arkansas stones. Sandpaper is also a fast and effective material for sharpening your tools.

We will use sandpaper in this book, but any of the stones will sharpen your tools. If you use a sharpening stone, follow the manufacturer's recommendation on how to use it.

Some sharpening materials cut faster than others. Also, some need water on the surface as you sharpen, some need oil, and some can be used dry, or without anything on the surface. It really doesn't matter what type of material you use. It's the technique that will get your tools sharp.

Whatever you choose, all sharpening materials contain some type of abrasive, called grit. Grit is what removes metal from your tools as you sharpen. The grit can be material such as diamond, silicon carbide, aluminum oxide, ceramic, or novaculite.

The size of the grit determines how fast metal is removed as you sharpen. The larger the grit size, the faster it will remove metal. Large, or coarse, grit will cut fast, but it leaves large scratches in the blade where it removed large amounts of metal. You will then need to go to finer and finer grits to remove these scratches and put sharp edges on your tools. A properly sharpened tool will have a blade so smooth that it looks like a mirror. The smooth surface will cut down the resistance of the tool blade as it slides through wood.

I recommend using sandpaper when you first start sharpening your tools because it is available in many different grits, is reasonably priced, and can be found at any hardware or home improvement store. By using various grits, you can go all the way from shaping to polishing the blades on your tools.

Diamond Plate

Oil Stone

Two-sided Water Stone

Two-sided Oil Stone

Make a Sandpaper Sharpening Tool

Using particleboard and sandpaper, you can easily make a sharpening tool that works great. You'll need a piece of particleboard that measures about 4½" by 11". If you don't have a piece that size, have an adult cut one for you.

Here's how to make the tool: Cut a sheet of 400-grit sandpaper in half, and use a glue stick to glue it to a flat piece of particleboard that's the same size as the paper.

When the sandpaper wears out, simply pull it off and replace it with a new piece.

If you don't have access to particleboard, glue sandpaper to paint stir sticks. This will give a smaller work area, but the tool will still work. Glue a different grit to each side of each stick.

How to Tell If a Knife Needs to Be Sharpened

Begin the sharpening process by testing your tool. A properly sharpened knife should have straight sides on the blade, should have a cutting edge so sharp you can't see it, should flow through wood easily, and should leave a smooth surface where you cut.

A good visual test is to look at the cutting edge in bright light; you should not be able to see the edge. If you see any reflections of light along the cutting edge, the blade is dull.

Here's another way to test your knife: Put on a carving glove and a thumb guard. Make a cut across the grain on a piece of wood to determine if the blade needs sharpening. If the knife cuts and leaves a smooth, shiny surface where it cut, you're ready to carve.

If the knife cuts but tears the wood, start with 600-grit sandpaper, and then strop. If it doesn't want to cut, start with 320-grit sandpaper. Then, move to 400 grit, 600 grit, and then strop. If the blade is dull or has nicks, you need to use 320 grit to start the sharpening process.

Skills: How to Sharpen a Knife

Before you begin sharpening, make sure you have prepared all of your materials. Make all of your sandpaper tools, or prepare your sharpening stones according to the manufacturer's directions.

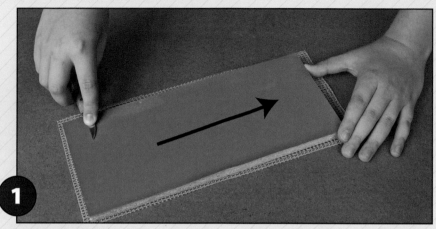

1

Position the Knife
Lay the knife blade flat on the right end of the sandpaper, with the blade cutting edge facing right. Place your pointer finger on the blade to keep the blade flat on the 320-grit sandpaper.

2

Sharpen One Side
Pull the knife from the right end to the left end of the sandpaper.

Continue Sharpening
Do this until the blade is properly shaped on this side.

Change Sides
Turn the blade over, and lay it flat on the left end of the sandpaper, with the cutting edge facing left.

Finish through the Grits
Pull the knife from the left end to the right end until the blade is properly shaped on this side. Once you have finished shaping the blade, go to 400-grit sandpaper, and do the same steps until all the coarse abrasions are removed from the blade. Then, go to 600-grit, and do the same until the blade begins to look polished. You are now ready to strop the blade.

Skills: How to Sharpen a Gouge

Approach the sharpening stone with the gouge as if you are going to carve the sharpening stone. When the tool touches the stone, you have the proper angle established.

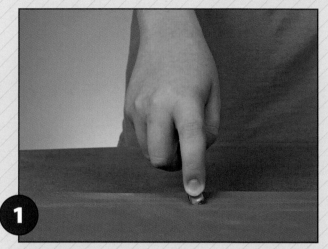

1

Lock Your Wrist
Lock your wrist to maintain the angle.

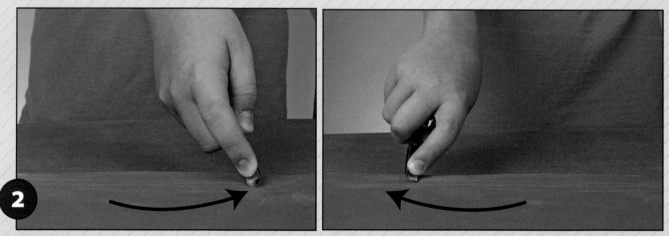

2

Sharpen
Slide the gouge back and forth across the stone. As you slide it, follow the contour of the gouge, rotating the gouge from one wing to the other.

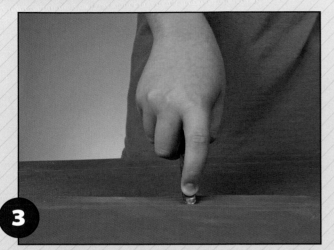

Form a Burr
Continue sliding the tool across the stone until you have a burr across the total inside of the gouge. (A burr is formed when the metal gets so thin that it starts to roll over.)

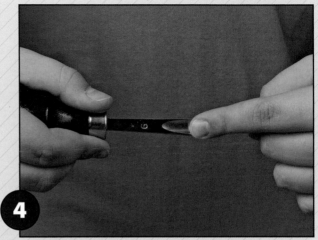

Check the Burr
To feel for a burr, carefully run your finger across the burr. Never run your finger into the cutting edge.

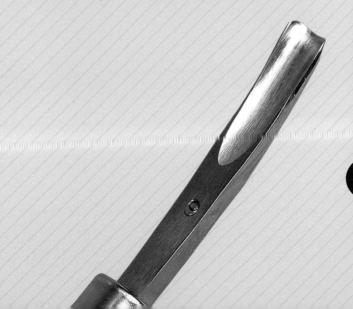

Remove the Burr
Fold a sheet of 600-grit sandpaper into quarters, and round it to fit the inside of the gouge. Pull the inside of the gouge across the sandpaper a few times until you can't feel the burr. Then, move on to stropping.

Skills: How to Sharpen a V-Tool

A V-tool is three tools in one. Each wing is a flat chisel, and the bottom of the V is a small gouge. When you sharpen, do it in three steps: each wing and then the small gouge.

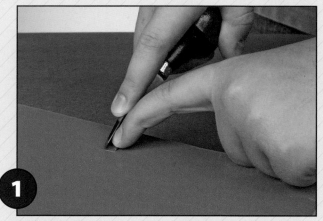

1

Set the Angle
Approach the stone with the left wing as if you are going to carve the stone. When you have the angle established, lock your wrist. Make sure the wing is flat on the sharpening stone.

2

Sharpen the Left Wing
Lay your pointer finger on the inside of the wing for control of the tool. Slide the wing back and forth across the stone, and check often to see where you're scraping the surface of the wing.

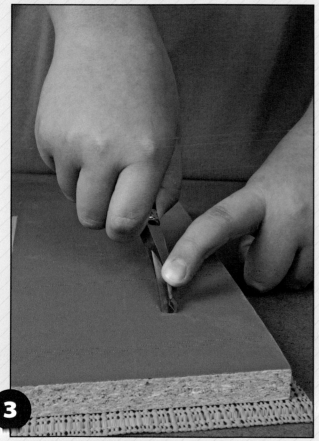

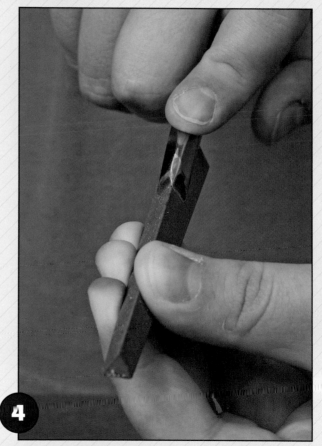

Sharpen the Right Wing

When the left wing is shaped, approach the stone as if you're going to carve it with the right wing. Lay your pointer finger on top of the left wing, and slide the wing back and forth across the stone. Once both wings are sharpened, sharpen the trough the same way you sharpened the gouge (page 60).

Remove Any Burrs

Test for burrs on the inside of the V-tool as you did with the gouge (page 61). If the inside of the V-tool has any burrs, lay the tool on an India taper triangle (page 69), and pull it across the surface to remove any burrs that may have formed in the sharpening process. Now you are ready to strop the blade.

Tools

Honing Compound

Honing compound is a very fine-grit abrasive that does the actual final sharpening and polishing of your tool's blade. There are many different types of honing compound. Some will put the razor edge on the blade and polish it faster than others, but any type will work. You rub honing compound on a strop to put a razor edge on your tools.

Examples of honing compound

Cardstock or paperboard for stropping a gouge or V-tool

Strop

A strop holds the honing compound on which you will rub your tool to sharpen it. Stropping is done after sharpening through the grits or to refresh the edge of your tool during carving. To strop your knife, you will use a leather strop. To strop your gouge and your V-tool, you will use a piece of cardboard from the back of a tablet or from the inside of a cereal box because it can be formed to the curved blades.

You can purchase a leather strop, or you can make your own. To make a leather strop, glue some leather that is about ⅛" thick (from something such as an old leather belt) to a piece of flat wood. A flat paint stir stick can make a great backer.

A leather strop

Skills: How to Strop a Knife

Gather all of your materials before you begin. Have your purchased or homemade leather strop and your honing compound ready.

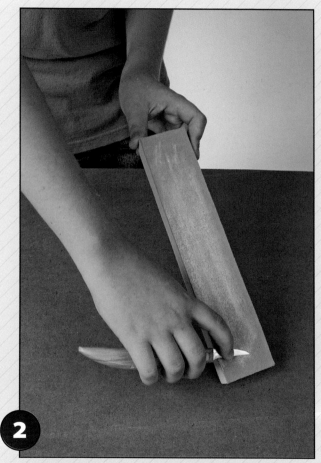

1

Apply Honing Compound
Rub honing compound into your strop. This is called "loading the strop."

2

Position the Knife
Hold the top end of the strop with your left hand. Lay the knife blade flat on the bottom of the strop, with the blade's cutting edge facing down. (Make sure the cutting edge is not close to your left hand.) Place your right-hand pointer finger on the blade.

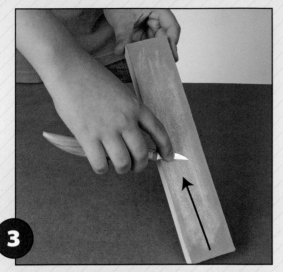

3

Strop

Pull the knife from the bottom to the top of the strop, keeping pressure on the blade with your right pointer finger. Repeat this about 8 to 10 times.

4

Do the Other Side

Turn the knife over to the other side of the blade. Lay the knife blade flat on the left end of the strop, with the blade's cutting edge facing left. Place your right-hand pointer finger on the blade.

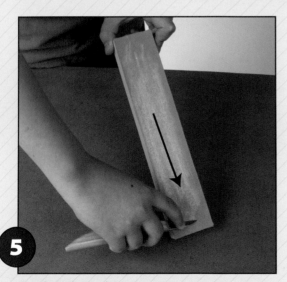

5

Continue Stropping

Pull the knife from the left end of the strop to the right end of the strop. Do this about 8 to 10 times.

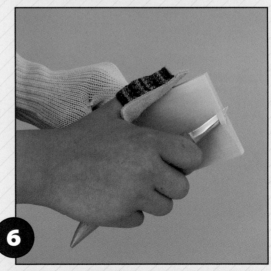

6

Make the Final Strokes

Strop each side a couple more times, and you should be ready to carve.

Skills: How to Strop a Gouge

Start with the outside of the gouge, and then move to the inside.

1

Apply Honing Compound
Rub honing compound into a piece of cardboard from the back of a tablet or the inside of a cereal box.

2

Strop the Outside
Lay the gouge on the cardboard strop. Rub it back and forth across the strop, following the contour of the gouge.

3

Strop the Inside
Roll the cardboard to fit the inside of the gouge. Then, place the gouge on the cardboard strop. Pull the gouge across the strop about five times. Now, you should be ready to carve.

Strop Frequently

All wood contains some abrasive materials, so your tools will dull slowly as you carve. If after carving for a period of time, your tool doesn't cut as it did when you first sharpened it, strop the blade again. Stropping should put the sharp edge back on the tool. If after stropping, it still doesn't cut properly, go to 600-grit sandpaper to shape the cutting edge of the blade and then to your strop.

Skills: How to Strop a V-tool

As with the gouge, strop the outside of the V-tool first, and then move to the inside edge. When you're finished, the V-tool should flow through the wood easily and leave a smooth, shiny surface where it cut.

1

Apply Honing Compound
Rub honing compound into a piece of cardboard from the back of a tablet or the inside of a cereal box.

2

Strop the Right Wing
Lay the right wing flat on the cardboard strop, and rub it back and forth across the strop.

3

Strop the Left Wing
Lay the left wing flat on the cardboard strop, and rub it back and forth. Then, strop the gouge portion by rubbing it back and forth across the strop, following the contour of the gouge.

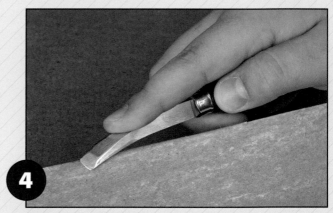

4

Strop the Inside Edges
Rub honing compound along one edge of the cardboard strop. Lay the inside of one of the wings over the edge of the cardboard, and pull it toward you. Do this about five times. Then, do the same for the other wing.

India Taper Triangle

This tool is specially shaped to remove any burrs, or wire edges, from the inside of a V-tool. It has a 60° angle for V-tools with angles 60° or greater. For V-tools with angles less than 60°, there are other tools, called slip stones, which have tighter tapers.

Things to Remember as You Carve

- As you do a carving, take your time and don't rush.

- Always have control of your tools. Remember, they are not toys; they are very sharp and can cut you quickly.

- Think about each cut you're going to make before you make it. Ask yourself: Where are my hands? Are they in a safe place if the tool slips? What do I want to accomplish with the cut I'm going to make?

- Make shallow cuts. You have much more control doing shallow cuts than trying to remove too much wood as you cut.

- Don't get distracted. Concentrate on what you are doing.

- If your hands or arms get tired, take a break. Put your knife down and relax for a while.

- Most of all, have fun. Enjoy carving, because it's fun making things with wood.

Brushes

Brushes are not only for painting. You'll need brushes for cleaning dust and wood chips from your carvings. You will also want some brushes for applying varnish.

Toothbrush

A new or used toothbrush works great to clean chips from your carvings. The bristles are stiff enough to get into tight areas but not abrasive enough to scar the carving.

Paintbrushes

Paintbrushes are available in many styles and with many types of hair or bristles. Whatever type you choose, make sure they are high-quality brushes. Good brushes will retain their shape and allow you to control the paint application. Cheap brushes tend to lose bristles and leave brush marks in the paint.

Paintbrushes can have other uses, too. Try using a wide paintbrush for brushing dust and chips from your work area. You may also want a slightly larger brush for applying varnish.

CHAPTER 4
Projects

Soap Boat

Carving soap is an excellent way to learn how to carve. Because we are using soap for this project instead of wood, we do not need sharp tools, but we will use the same basic techniques used for carving wood.

The best soap for carving is Ivory bar soap. It is inexpensive and easy to carve. Plus, it floats—so your finished boat will, too. Ivory bar soap comes in two sizes. We will use the large bar, which is 4½ ounces, but either size will work. Use only soap that is in its original wrapper, and do not unwrap it until you're ready to carve, so it doesn't dry out.

Note to Adults

This is a great project for you to assist a young person in making some tools to carve soap and then observe how he or she uses the tools. Impress upon your pupil to use the tools as if they were real carving tools and to follow all safety procedures required when using sharp tools. If he or she shows the maturity and dexterity required to use sharp carving tools, the next project could be the snowman ornament (page 78), which is made using real carving tools.

Tools

Large cookie sheet or large piece of freezer paper

Felt-tip marker

Homemade wooden craft stick knife or heavy duty plastic knife

Homemade wooden gouge

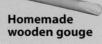

Scissors

Carving Pattern: Soap Boat

Materials
- 4½-ounce bar of Ivory soap

Supplies
- Straw (for the mast)
- Piece of cardboard (for the sail)
- Rubber band

Skills
- Measuring and Marking, page 30
- Pull Cut, page 44
- Push Cut, page 45
- Stop Cut, page 47
- Gouge Cut, page 51

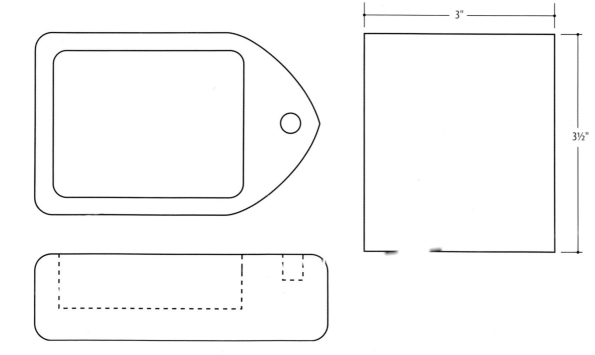

3"

3½"

Make Your Own Soap-Carving Tools

These tools are easy to make and are perfect for carving soap. We will make a knife from wooden craft sticks and a gouge from a wooden dowel.

Gouge

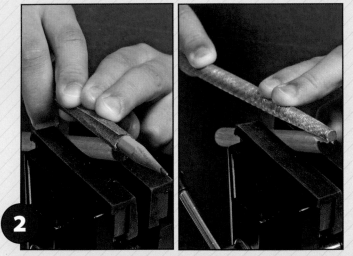

1

To make the gouge, cut a ½" diameter dowel about 5" to 6½" long. Use coarse sandpaper to sand off about half the diameter along one end of the dowel.

You'll Need:
- About four wooden craft sticks
- ½" wooden dowel
- Backsaw
- Vise
- Coarse sandpaper
- Yellow wood glue
- Clamp
- Fine sandpaper
- Red marker

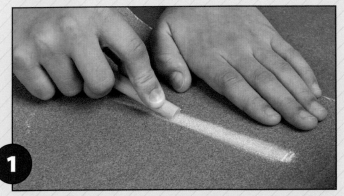

2

Use a red marker to color the sanded end of the dowel. Mount the dowel in a vise. Remove wood from the sanded end of the dowel using a round rasp or coarse sandpaper wrapped around a pencil.

3

Remove wood from the inside of the gouge until all of the red is gone. Sand the inside and outside of the gouge with fine sandpaper, and you have a handy gouge.

Knife

1 Put the craft stick in a vise and cut off one end using a backsaw.

2 Shape the cut end of the stick, as shown, by pulling it across coarse sandpaper.

3 Continue to pull the stick across coarse sandpaper to shape both sides of the cut end and make the cutting edge of the knife. The cutting edge should be about 1½" long.

4 Hold one of the craft sticks in your hand to see what length feels comfortable. Mark one end to be cut to the length you measured. Cut the four wooden craft sticks and sand the cut ends slightly so they are smooth. Spread glue on all surfaces of the sticks, except the two outside surfaces. The order should be two of the handle sticks, the stick with the knife blade and the piece that you cut off, and then the other two handle sticks. Clamp the sticks together until the glue dries.

Making: Soap Boat

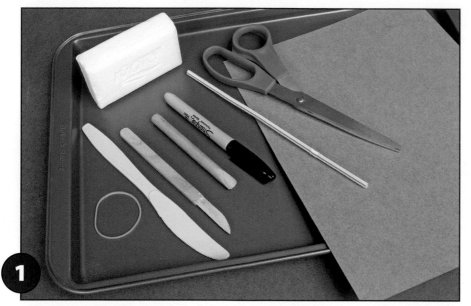

1

Set Up Your Work Area
To contain the soap chips and make cleanup easier, carve on a large cookie sheet or a large piece of freezer paper. Don't use newspaper, because the print will come off on the soap.

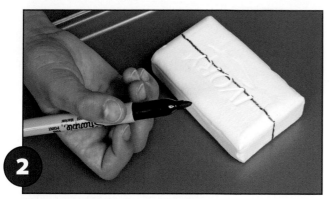

2

Draw a Centerline
Using a felt-tip marker, draw a line down the center of the bar of soap. This line will be a reference point so you can make sure that both sides of the boat are contoured the same. Extend the line down the ends and across the bottom.

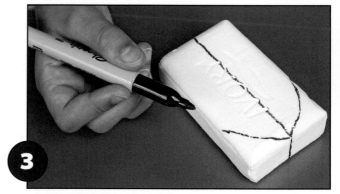

3

Draw in the Bow
Draw a rounded edge that is about even on both sides.

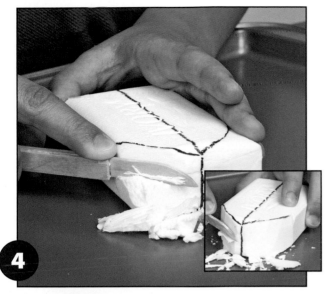

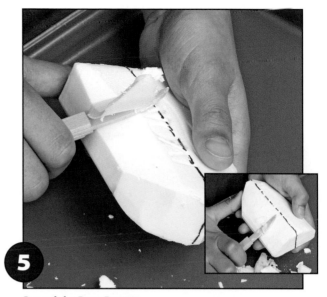

Shape the Bow
Use a homemade wooden knife or a heavy-duty plastic knife to remove soap from both sides of the bow. Lay the soap flat on your work surface, and slice off the soap from both sides of the bow.

Round the Boat Bottom
Use pull cuts to shape the bottom of the boat. Remove the same amount of soap from both sides.

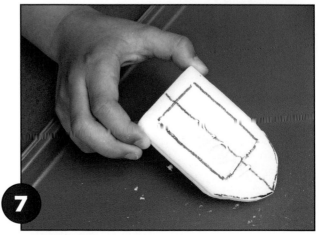

Smooth the Bow
Use push cuts to shape and smooth the bow.

Mark the Inside
Draw where you will remove material to shape the inside of the boat. It should be a rectangular shape.

Making: Soap Boat

8

Carve the Inside
With a homemade wooden gouge, remove soap from the inside of the boat. Be careful not to remove too much, or you will go through the bottom of the boat.

9

Straighten the Inside Walls
Use the knife to cut straight sides on the inside of your boat.

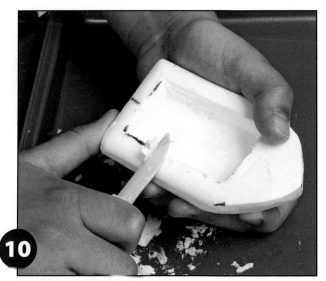

10

Smooth the Top Surface
Use pull cuts to flatten the top of the boat.

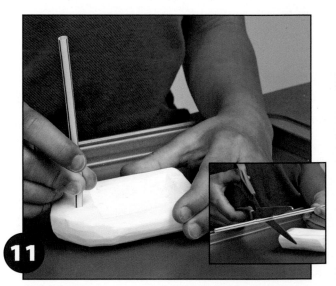

11

Make the Mast
With scissors, cut a straw about 5" long. Then, push one end of the straw into the bow of the boat.

12

Cut the Sail
Using scissors, cut a sail about 3" by 3½" out of cardboard.

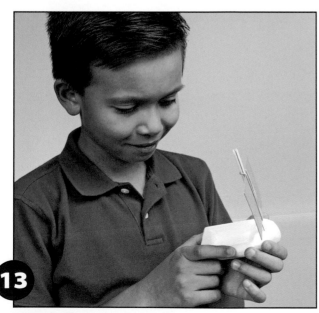

13

Attach the Sail
Attach the sail to the mast using a rubber band.

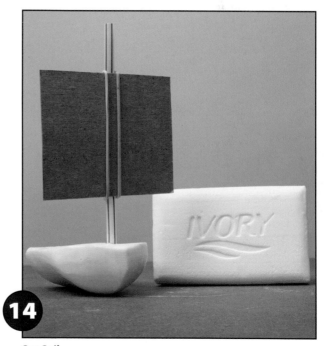

14

Set Sail
You started with a bar of soap and now have a boat ready to sail. All you need is some water and a little wind power from you.

Snowman Ornament

This snowman is a nice carving anyone would be happy to hang on a Christmas tree or just for display. The project is also a great way to learn about wood grain. We discussed wood grain as we learned about wood's anatomy in Chapter 1. Your knife should never be given the opportunity to go between vessels, because the wood will split. In this project, you will see why you need to always cut across the wood grain and not into it. Each cut must be in the right direction, or you could easily chip off pieces you want to keep.

We will also drill holes for the nose and the hanger. The nose will be carved separately and inserted into the hole you drilled in the face. We'll complete the carving by painting it.

Tools

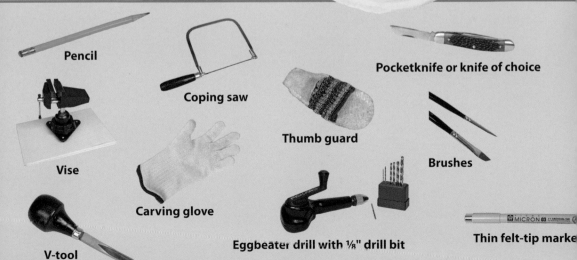

Pencil

Coping saw

Pocketknife or knife of choice

Thumb guard

Brushes

Vise

Carving glove

V-tool

Eggbeater drill with ⅛" drill bit

Thin felt-tip marker

Carving Pattern: Snowman Ornament

Materials
- Basswood block, ¼" thick by 3" wide by 4½" long

Supplies
- Carbon paper
- Masking tape
- Nonslip material
- Small container
- Acrylic paints (white, black, red, green, and yellow)
- Wax paper
- Yellow wood glue
- String

Skills
- Transferring a Pattern, page 17
- Making Curved Cuts, page 35
- Removing Wood with a V-Tool, page 53
- Pull Cut, page 44
- Push Cut, page 45
- Drilling Holes, page 37
- Score Cut, page 48
- Painting, page 22

Projects

Making: Snowman Ornament

1

2

Prepare for Pattern Transfer
Place a piece of carbon paper between the front pattern and the block of wood. Tape the pattern to the piece of wood at the top.

Transfer the Pattern
Using a pencil, trace over the lines to draw the pattern on the wood.

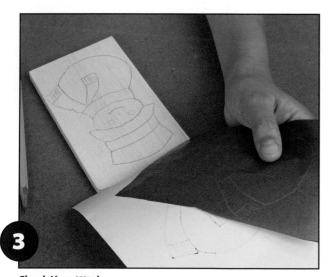

3

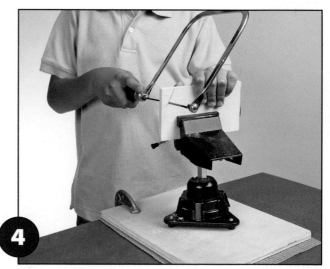

4

Check Your Work
By taping only at the top of the pattern, you can easily check to see if you've traced the entire pattern.

Clamp and Cut
Clamp the piece of wood in a vise, and carefully cut out the blank with a coping saw. Save a small piece of scrap wood for the snowman's nose.

5

Remove Lines with the V-tool
Lay the blank you just cut on some nonslip material, and use a V-tool to remove all of the lines you traced on the blank. Make sure an adult is supervising as you carve.

6

Cut the Fringes
Cut the fringes on the ends of the scarf with the V-tool.

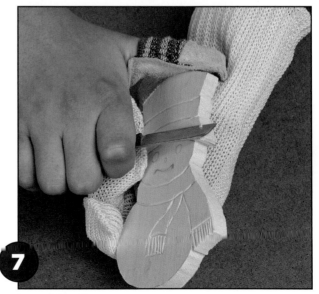

7

Round the Edges
Put on a carving glove and a thumb guard. Then, with a knife, use pull cuts and push cuts to round the outside edges of the snowman. Always cut in the direction of the grain so your knife will not go between the grain. If your knife wants to go between the grain, cut in the other direction. You want a smooth surface where you cut.

Making: Snowman Ornament

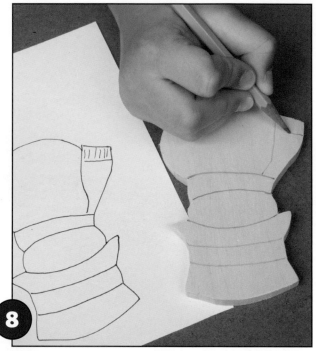

8

Draw the Back Pattern Freehand

Turn the snowman over, and using the back pattern, draw it by hand. Using your V-tool, remove all the lines you just drew. Then, put on your carving glove and thumb guard, and, using your knife, round off the edges on this side.

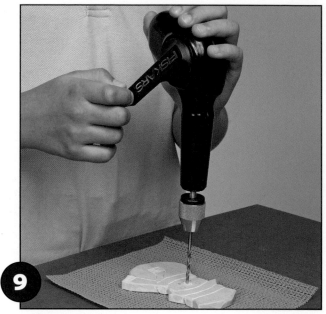

9

Drill Holes

Turn the snowman to his front side, and using an eggbeater drill with a ⅛" drill bit, drill a hole halfway through the wood where his nose will go. Then, drill a hole all the way through the wood, near the top of his hat. This hole will be used to put string through so the snowman can be displayed.

10

Carve the Nose

Put on your carving glove and thumb guard. To make the nose, use pull cuts to round the small piece of scrap wood that you saved when you cut out the blank.

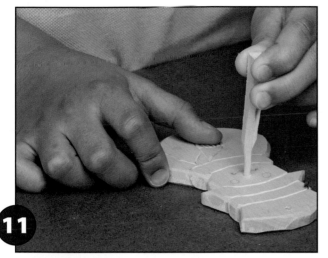

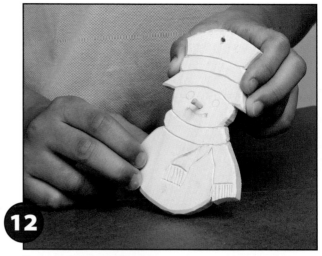

Fit and Cut the Nose

Make sure the nose fits in the hole, and then, use a score cut to cut the nose to the proper length.

Remove Chips and Dust

Brush away any chips or dust, and your snowman is ready to be painted. Set his nose to the side in a safe place. You'll paint it before you insert it into his face.

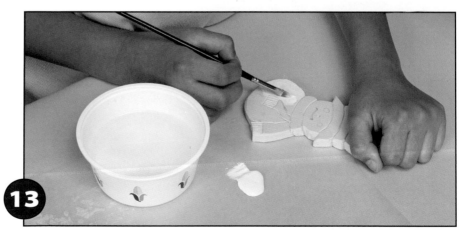

Paint the Face and Body

Fill a small container about half full of water for washing brushes, and spread a small bead of white paint on some wax paper. The wax paper will be your palette and protect your working surface. Paint the face and the body on the snowman's front and back with the white paint. Wash the white paint from the brush. Make sure the paint is dry on one side of your snowman before moving to the other side.

Making: Snowman Ornament

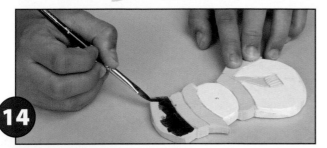

14

Paint the Hat and Scarf

Paint the hat on both the front and back with black paint. Wash the paint from your brush. Then, paint the hatband, scarf, and scarf tassels with whatever colors you want. This snowman will be painted with red and green.

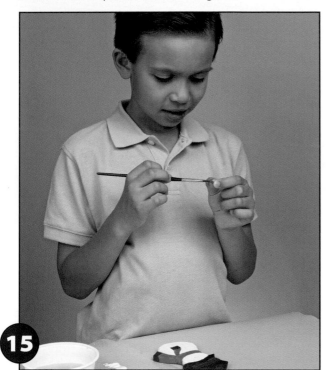

15

Paint the Nose

Mix a small amount of red and yellow paints to make orange for the carrot nose. Then, paint the nose.

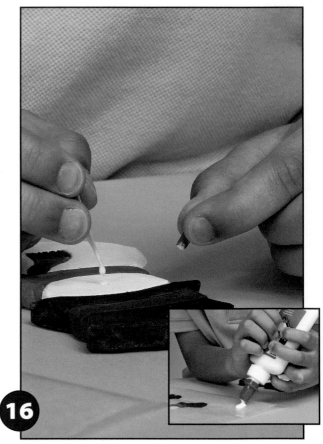

16

Apply Glue

Place a small drop of glue on the wax paper. Use a thin toothpick or a sliver of wood to place a small amount of glue in the hole for the nose.

Insert the Nose
Snugly press the nose into the drilled hole.

Draw the Eyes and Mouth
Use a thin felt-tip marker to draw in the eyes and mouth.

Attach the Hanger
Attach a string for the hanger. This is what your snowman should look like from the front and the back. Remember to put your name and the date on the back of your carving. Let everyone know it's your work.

Wooden Whistle

This is a fun project, and it makes a neat whistle. The carving can also be worn on a lanyard around your neck or made into a neckerchief slide.

You will need an experienced woodcarver or an adult to drill a hole ½" in diameter and 3½" deep in the piece to form the whistle cavity. A drill press with a ½" brad point bit works great for drilling the hole. A brad point bit has a center point that helps keep the bit drilling straight. Ask almost any woodworker, and he will have the tools to do this.

Make sure you read through the entire step-by-step section before you begin, because it includes several options for doing the different parts of the process.

Tools

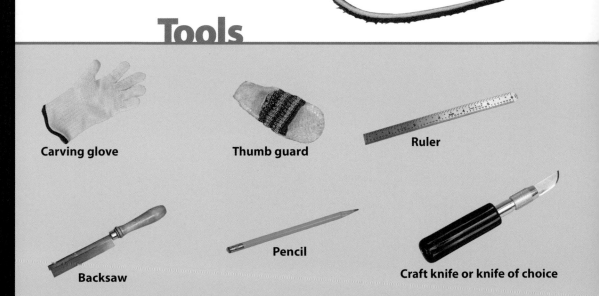

Carving glove

Thumb guard

Ruler

Backsaw

Pencil

Craft knife or knife of choice

Carving Pattern: Wooden Whistle

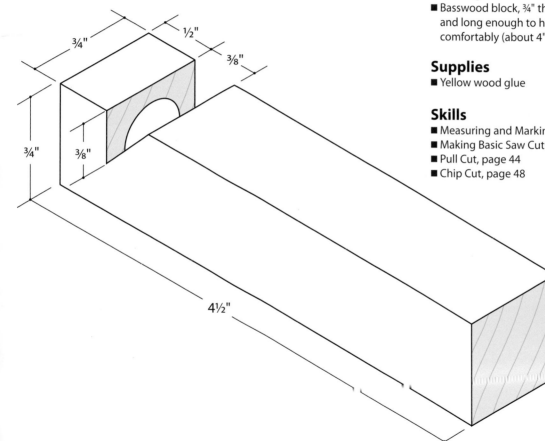

¾"

½"

⅜"

¾"

⅜"

4½"

Materials
- Basswood block, ¾" thick by ¾" wide by 4½" long
- Basswood block, ¾" thick by ¾" wide and long enough to hold comfortably (about 4" long)

Supplies
- Yellow wood glue

Skills
- Measuring and Marking, page 30
- Making Basic Saw Cuts, page 36
- Pull Cut, page 44
- Chip Cut, page 48

Making: Wooden Whistle

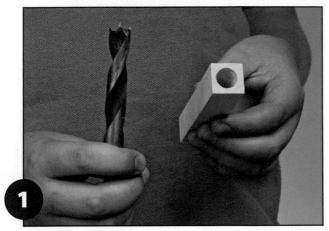

Get a Drilled Blank
Start with a piece of basswood ¾" thick by ¾" wide by 4½" long with a ½" hole drilled 3½" deep.

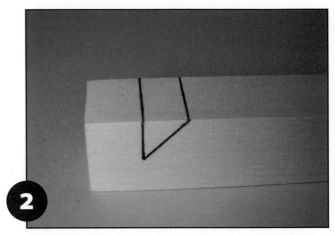

Measure and Mark
Using a pencil and a ruler, draw a line ½" from the open end of the piece. Draw another line ⅜" from the first line. Turn the piece on its side, and extend the first line ⅜" onto the side. Draw a line from the second line down to meet the extension of the first line on the side of the piece.

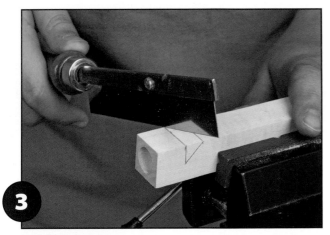

Saw the First Line
Using a backsaw, cut across the first line down to the bottom of the mark.

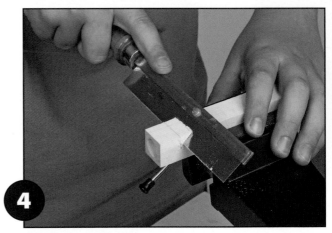

Saw the Second Line.
Tilt the backsaw and saw the second line to remove the whistle hole.

Option: Cut the Whistle Hole with a Knife

You can also cut out the whistle hole using a knife. Remember to wear your carving glove and thumb guard.

1

Make stop cuts (page 47).

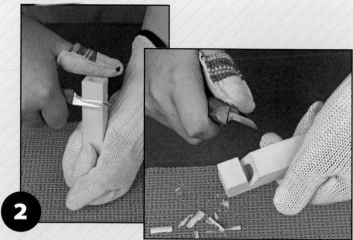

2

Remove wood up to the stop cuts until the hole is the required depth (page 52).

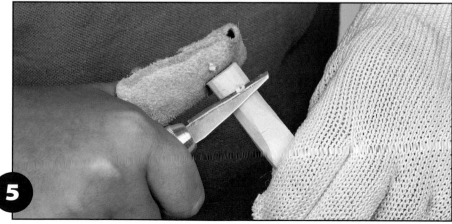

5

Start the Plug
Put on a carving glove and a thumb guard to make a plug for the mouthpiece hole with a craft knife. You'll need a piece of basswood that's ¾" thick by ¾" wide, and about 4" long so it's comfortable to hold as you round one end.

Projects

Making: Wooden Whistle

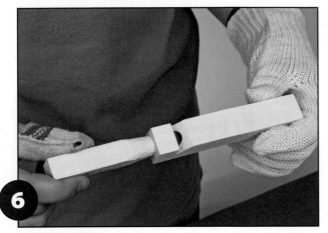

6

Round the Plug
Using small pull cuts, round the plug to fit the hole at the mouthpiece. The rounded area should be at least ¾" long.

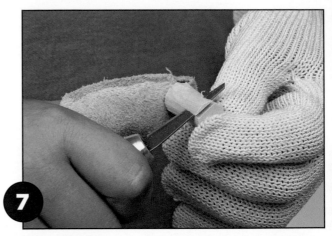

7

Carve a Flat Area
When you have the plug round and it fits snugly inside the hole, remove it. Then, cut the plug 1" long so ½" of it sticks out of the mouthpiece. Carve a flat area on the plug. You might want to cut the plug longer so that if the whistle doesn't work, you can easily remove the plug to make a larger flat spot.

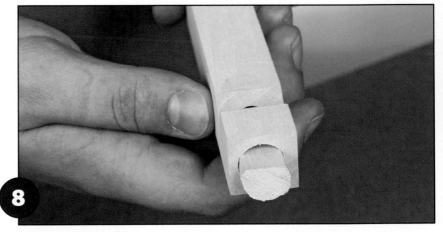

8

Adjust the Plug to Fit
Insert the plug in the hole up to the vertical cut in the whistle. The flat area should be facing up. Test the whistle. It should make a neat whistle sound.

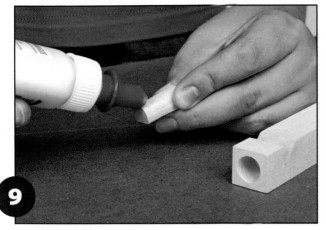

9

Apply Glue
When the whistle works, remove the plug. Spread a small amount of glue on the round surface.

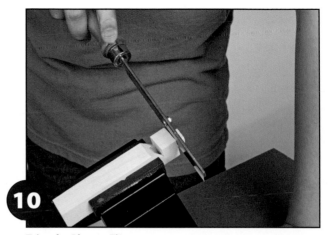

10

Trim the Plug to Fit
Insert the plug back into the whistle, with the flat side facing up. Once the glue has dried, cut the plug flush with the end of the mouthpiece using the backsaw.

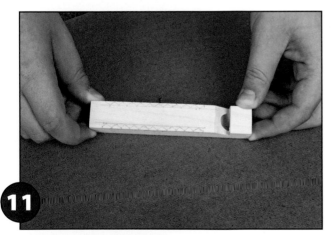

11

Measure and Mark the Design
Measure back ¼" from the whistle hole, and make small marks every ¼" for 3" on both sides of the whistle.

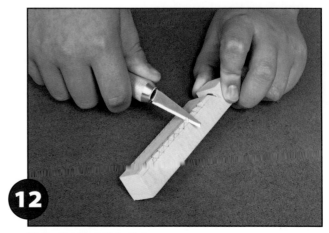

12

Make the First Chip Cut
Tilt your knife about 45°, and starting with the first line, cut down halfway to the next line.

Making: Wooden Whistle

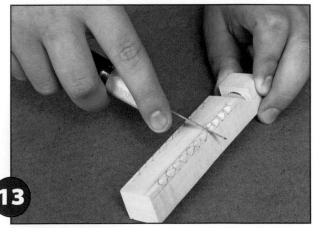

13

Make the Second Cut
Tilt your knife 45° the other way, and remove the chip.

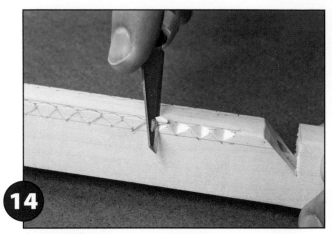

14

Make the Final Cut
Slice along the bottom of the triangle to release the chip. It should look like this. Repeat the chip carving on both of the top sides.

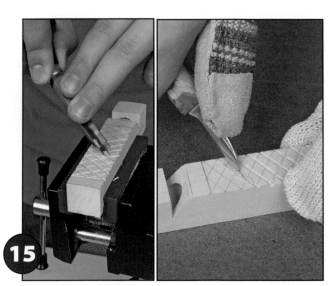

15

Try a Different Design
You can also try this interesting design. Draw a crosshatch pattern every ¼" on the whistle, and remove the lines with a V-tool or a knife. Be sure to cut with the knife at a 45° angle on both sides of the line.

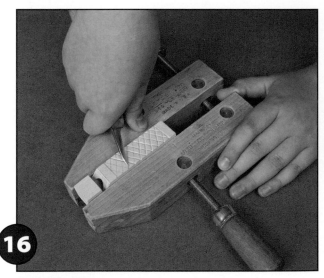

16

Clamp the Piece
If you prefer not holding the piece, it can be clamped while you carve with your knife.

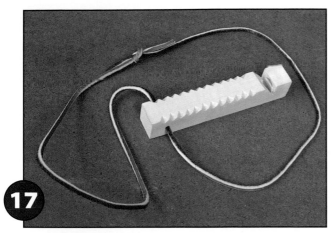

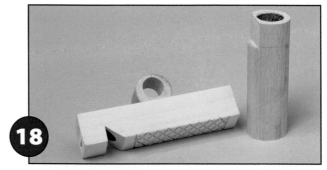

17

Attach a Lanyard

Drill a hole through the end of the whistle and attach a lanyard so the whistle can be worn around your neck. Make sure the hole is not drilled through the hole in the center of the whistle chamber. If you drill a hole through the sound chamber, the whistle will not work.

18

Try a Neckerchief Slide

Add a neckerchief slide by drilling a ½" hole in a large dowel, sawing a flat on one side of the dowel, and cutting it ⅝" long. Glue the slide to the whistle.

19

Allow the Glue to Dry

Don't disturb the piece while the glue dries and bonds the whistle and slide together. When the glue dries, the whistle makes an attractive slide.

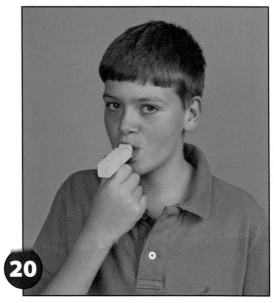

20

Test the Whistle

Your whistle is now complete. Whatever type you make, it will have a neat sound.

Projects

Arrowhead

You can do many things with a carving like this. It can be used for a neckerchief slide, a spearhead, or a pendant. If you make a neckerchief slide, carve only one side and attach a slide to the back of the carving. If you make a spearhead, carve both sides and tie it to a shaft using a leather lace. Use beads to enhance the carving. To make a pendant, use a leather lace and some beads for decoration. You can also make a nametag by carving or writing your name on the front of the carving.

The suggestions here are just a few of the options. See how many ways you can think to use this arrowhead. Be sure to read through the entire step-by-step instructions before you begin, and then decide which project you'd like to make.

Try using varnish for this project. It will bring out the beauty of the butternut wood grain.

Tools

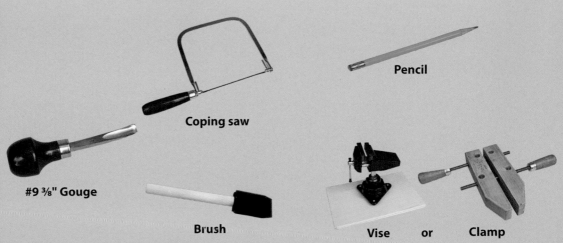

Coping saw

Pencil

#9 ⅜" Gouge

Brush

Vise   or   **Clamp**

Carving Pattern: Arrowhead

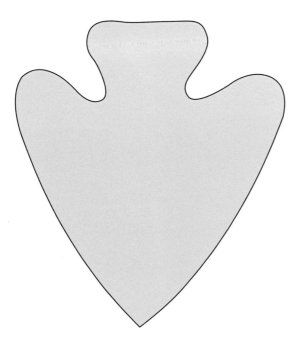

Materials
- Butternut block, ¼" thick by 3" wide by 3" long (you could use any type of wood, but butternut has a beautiful grain pattern)

Supplies
- Scrap wood
- Nonslip material
- Glue (optional)
- Varnish (optional)

Skills
- Transferring a Pattern, page 17
- Making Curved Cuts, page 35
- Gouge Cut, page 51
- Varnishing, page 23

Making: Arrowhead

1

Make a Template
Make a template to lay out the arrowhead. Have the wood grain running the length of the carving.

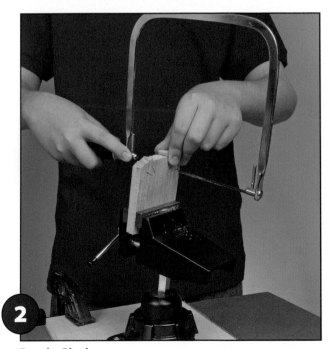

2

Saw the Blank
Clamp the piece of wood in a vise, and use a coping saw to cut out the arrowhead. This is the blank.

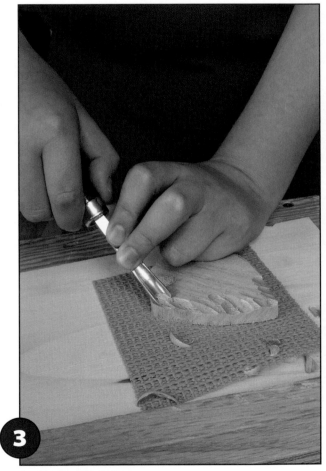

3

Set Up Your Work Area
Place a piece of scrap wood under some nonslip material. When you make cuts around the arrowhead, the gouge will go into the scrap material rather than into the bench or table upon which you are carving. Lay the blank on the nonslip material.

4

Round the Arrowhead
Use a gouge to shape the arrowhead. Make cuts so it looks as if pieces have been chipped off the edges, just as the edges of a real arrowhead look. Always cut across the grain so you don't split the wood. If your gouge wants to go between the grain, cut in the other direction.

5

Carve the Entire Surface
Go over the entire surface to give it a chipped appearance.

6

Make the Spearhead, Neckerchief, or Pendant
If you want to make a spearhead, carve both sides of the blank. If you're making a neckerchief slide or a pendant, only carve around the edges of the back. Then, carve or write your name on the arrowhead so everyone knows who carved it.

Making: Arrowhead

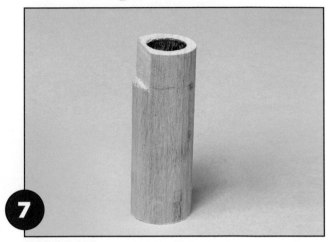

7

Make the Slide

You can make your own neckerchief slide by drilling a ⅝ or ¾" hole in the end of a dowel. Simply saw a flat on one side of the dowel, and then cut a piece about ⅝" long.

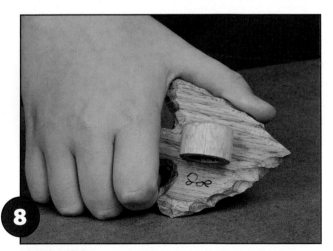

8

Glue the Slide

If you made a neckerchief slide, glue the slide to the back of the arrowhead.

9

Varnish the Carving

To protect the arrowhead, apply varnish. You can use a disposable brush (shown here) or a regular brush. If you varnish your carving, have an adult assist you, and make sure it's done in a well-ventilated area. Always follow the manufacturer's instructions on how to use the varnish. Once the varnish is dry, the arrowhead is complete.

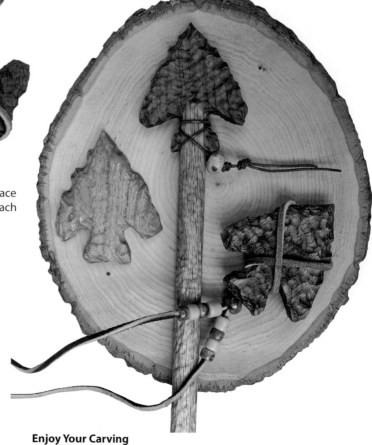

Finish with Beads and Leather

To make the spearhead or pendant, use some leather lace and beads, which are available at most craft shops. Attach them as shown in the photos.

Enjoy Your Carving

And don't forget to try your own variations of this project.

Projects

Name Plaque

Make a name plaque for your room. Carving it will give you practice in laying out a project, using a square, and using a gouge, a knife, and a V-tool. Most of all, it will teach you how to use the wood grain so you get smooth cuts.

You will do gouge cuts for the border, knife cuts for the letters and the chip carving, and V-tool cuts for the letters.

Tools

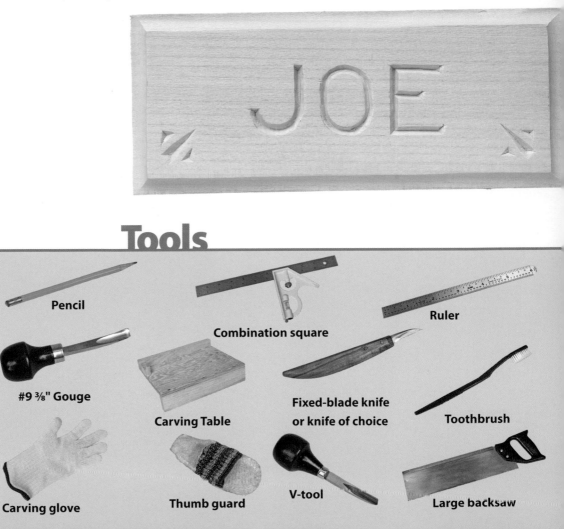

Pencil

Combination square

Ruler

#9 ⅜" Gouge

Carving Table

Fixed-blade knife or knife of choice

Toothbrush

Carving glove

Thumb guard

V-tool

Large backsaw

Carving Pattern: Name Plaque

Materials
- Basswood board, ¾" thick by 2½" wide by 3½" long, plus 1" for each letter you will carve.
- Allow 1¾" on the left end plus 1" for each letter you will carve.
- On the right end, you need 1¾" plus 2 extra inches. Once we have all the letters carved, we will cut off the excess.

Supplies
- Nonslip material
- 320-grit Sandpaper

Skills
- Measuring and Marking, page 30
- Gouge Cut, page 51
- Making Basic Saw Cuts, page 36
- Removing Wood to a Stop Cut, page 52
- Removing Wood with a V-tool, page 53
- Chip Cut, page 48

Making: Name Plaque

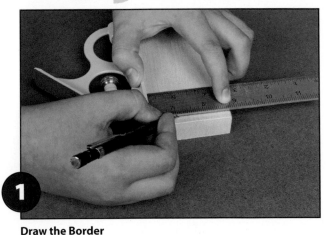

Draw the Border
Using a pencil and a combination square or a ruler, draw a line ¼" from one end and both the top and the bottom of the board.

Working with the Grain

Carefully look at the board to see which direction the grain runs. Along the top, this piece must be cut from the right to the left. On the bottom, it must be cut from left to right. If you were to cut in the opposite direction, the tool would attempt to go between the grain, and the wood would split into the area you want to save. If your gouge attempts to go between the grain, you are cutting in the wrong direction. You won't have to worry about this problem on the ends because you're cutting across the grain.

Carve the Border
Place the board on a carving table. Use a #9 ⅜" gouge to remove wood up to the lines. The wood should curl off like this.

Complete the Border Carving
Only cut up to the lines that form the border. When the border is carved on three sides, it should look like this.

Measure and Mark for the Letters
Measure in ¾" from the top and the bottom, and draw lines. Then, measure over 1¾" from the end with the carved border. Use the square to mark off the letters you will carve.

Draw the Letters
In the ¾" box, draw each letter. The letters will be ¾" wide, with ¼" between each letter. The bodies of the individual letters should be ⅛" wide.

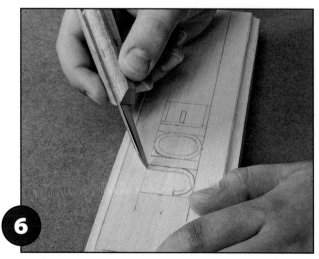

Make Stab Cuts
Using a fixed-blade knife, make stab cuts at the ends of the letters that have exposed ends. The O, for example, does not have an exposed end. To do this, tilt the knife handle about 45° away from the end of the letter and make the stab cut.

Making: Name Plaque

7

Start Carving the Letters
Using a V-tool, carefully remove wood between the letter lines. Start from the middle of the letter, and cut up to the stop cut. The piece should fall out. Be extra careful when doing curved areas—for example, on the J and the O.

8

Complete the Letters
Cut from the other direction to complete the letter. Do this on each of the letters.

9

Clean the Letters
Use a toothbrush to remove any chips.

10

Measure and Mark the Board End
Measure 1¾" from the last letter, and draw a line. Use the square to mark a straight line where you want to cut.

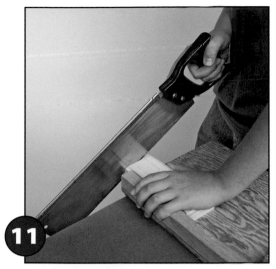

Saw the Waste Wood
Carefully cut off the waste wood from the end of your plaque with a large backsaw.

Cut the Final Border Side
Measure ¼" from the end you just cut, and cut the border. It should now look like this.

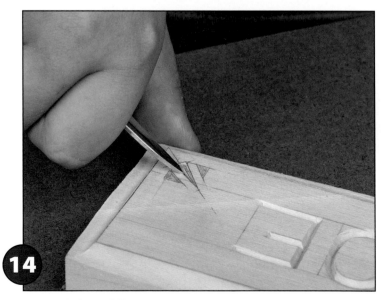

Measure and Mark the Chip Carving Pattern
To draw a chip carving design on your plaque, place the square at a 45° angle from the bottom right corner, and draw a 1"-long line. Draw the pattern on both bottom sides.

Start with the Middle Piece
Place the plaque on nonslip material. Tilt your knife and make a 45° angle cut at the end of the middle piece you will remove.

Making: Name Plaque

Carve the Second Side

Tilt the knife at a 45° angle on the other side of the chip. Pull the knife from the top to the bottom of the chip. The piece should fall out. If it doesn't, place the knife back in the cuts, and make them again until the piece falls out. Chip carve all of the pieces.

Carve the First Side

Using chip carving cuts, tilt your knife 45°, and cut from the top of the design to the bottom of it. The cut should start at the top of the darkened area and get deeper as you proceed to the bottom of the first cut you made. Notice how deep the knife angle is at the end of the cut.

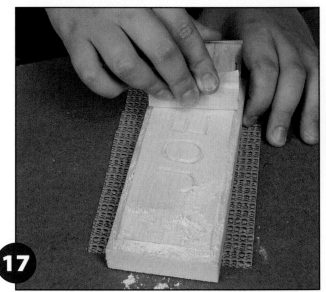

Sand the Plaque

After all of the cuts have been made, wrap a piece of sandpaper around a small block of wood, and sand off the pencil lines.

18

Remove the Dust
Use a toothbrush to remove the dust you created by sanding.

19

Use the Plaque
The result should look like this, except it should have your name on the plaque.

Projects

Eagle Head

This majestic eagle will be a definite conversation piece that you will be proud to show others. It is a nice relief carving, it is easy to do, and it will give you good practice using various tools.

Relief carving is a type of carving where the object is formed by removing wood to create shadows. Keep this in mind as you carve the eagle, and it will help you make it look real.

Tools

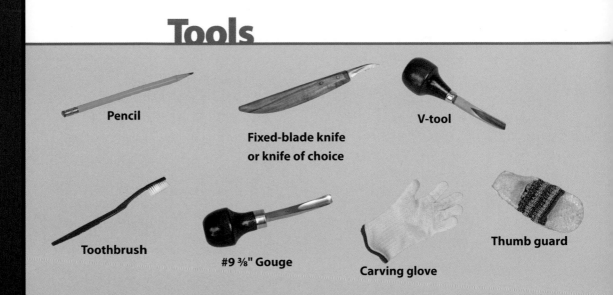

Pencil

Fixed-blade knife or knife of choice

V-tool

Toothbrush

#9 ⅜" Gouge

Carving glove

Thumb guard

Carving Pattern: Eagle Head

Materials
- Basswood board, ¾" thick by 5" wide by 6" long

Supplies
- Graphite paper
- Masking tape
- Nonslip material
- Graphic or carbon paper

Skills
- Transferring a Pattern, page 17
- Removing Wood with a V-tool, page 53
- Gouge Cut, page 51
- Removing Wood to a Stop Cut, page 52
- Pull Cut, page 44

Projects

Making: Eagle Head

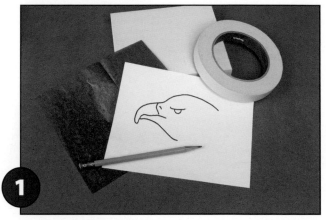

1

Gather the Materials
To trace the pattern onto the board, you will need the pattern, graphic or carbon paper, masking tape, and a pencil.

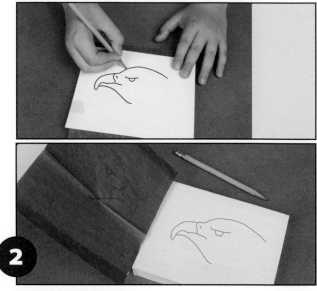

2

Trace the Pattern
Attach the pattern to the board on one end, and trace the pattern. Check your work to make sure you traced all of the lines before removing the pattern.

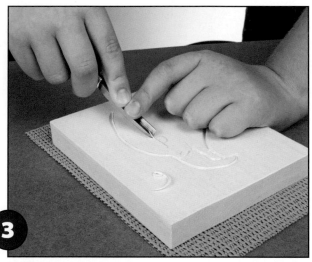

3

Outline with Your V tool
Place the board on nonslip material. Outline the head and beak with a V-tool. Carefully remove the line above the eye.

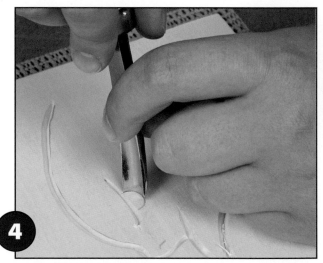

4

Outline the Eye Carefully
Outline the eye with a #9 ⅜" gouge. Carefully sink the gouge straight into the wood, and follow the contour of the gouge to outline the entire eye.

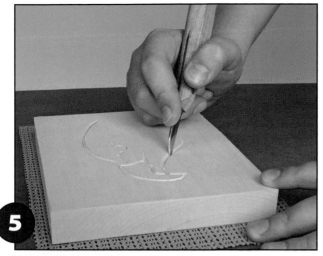

Deepen the Cuts
Use a fixed-blade knife to make a stop cut and deepen the area removed with the V-tool.

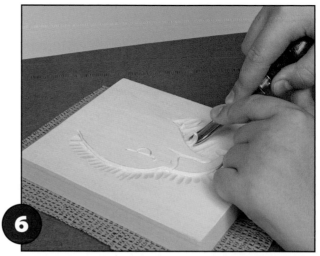

Remove the Background
Remove wood with the gouge all around the head up to the stop cut.

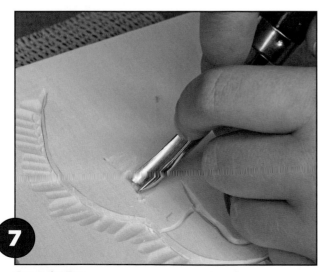

Carve the Eye
Carefully remove wood up to the stop cut over the eye.

Deepen the Stop Cut
Deepen the stop cut that forms the eye.

Projects

Making: Eagle Head

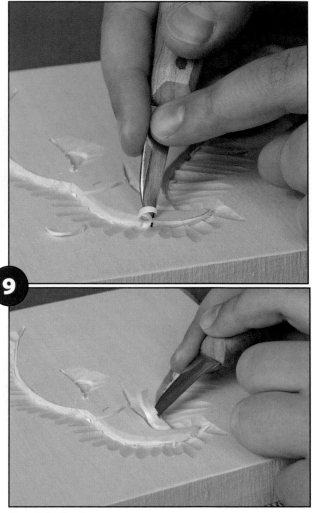

9

10

Clean the Carving
Clean loose chips from the carving with a toothbrush.

Shape the Beak
Using the knife, round the top beak. Remove wood from the bottom beak so it looks as if it is behind the top beak.

11

Create the Nostril
Use your V-tool to form the nostril.

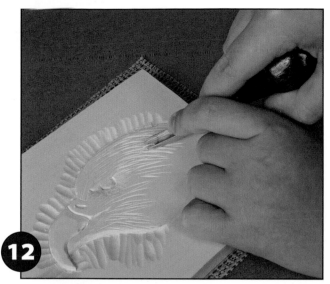

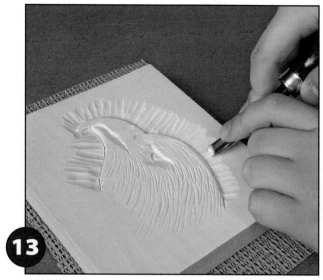

Make the Head Feathers
Form the flowing head feathers with your V-tool.

Set Off the Head
Remove more wood from around the head to make it look as if it sits off the board.

Finish the Eagle Head
Your finished eagle head should look like this. You can leave the carving without a finish, varnish it, or paint it.

Projects

Frog

This is a musical frog—when you rub the stick along the frog's back, it makes a croaking sound. It will make a different sound depending on which direction you rub the stick along its back.

If it is sitting out, this frog is a toy that people will not be able to pass by without trying it to see what sounds it makes.

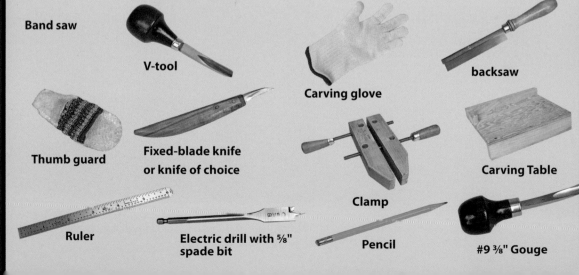

Tools

Band saw

V-tool

Carving glove

backsaw

Thumb guard

Fixed-blade knife or knife of choice

Clamp

Carving Table

Ruler

Electric drill with ⅝" spade bit

Pencil

#9 ⅜" Gouge

Carving Pattern: Frog

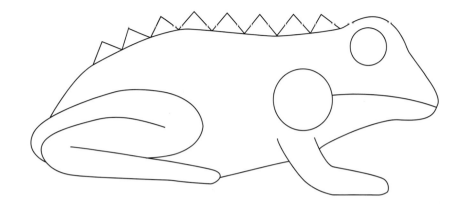

Materials
- Basswood blank, 1½" wide by 2" high by 4 ½" long
- ⅝"-diameter dowel, about 5" long

Supplies
- 220- and 320-grit sandpaper
- Acrylic paints (green and black)
- Gloss spray varnish

Skills
- Transferring a Pattern, page 17
- Measuring and Marking, page 30
- Making Basic Saw Cuts, page 36
- Push Cut, page 45
- Pull Cut, page 44
- Gouge Cut, page 52
- Removing Wood with a V-tool, page 53
- Removing Wood to a Stop Cut, page 52
- Sanding and Cleaning a Carving, page 15
- Painting, page 22

Projects

Making: Frog

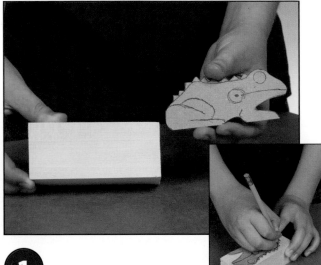

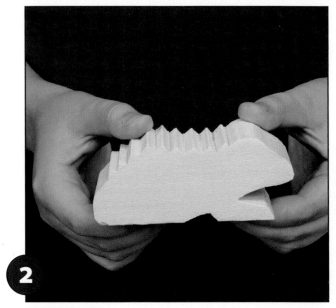

1

Transfer the Pattern
Make a template for the frog, and with a pencil, draw the pattern on the block of wood.

2

Saw the Blank
I recommend you find someone with a band saw to cut out the blank. If you do not have someone who can band saw the project for you, use a coping saw yourself.

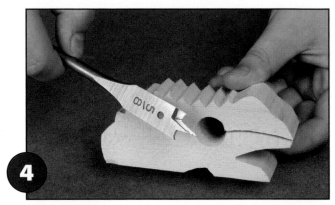

3

Draw the Mouth
Mark where the center of the drill hole will be, and draw in the mouth. Use a coping saw to cut the mouth into the carving or…

4

Drill the Hole
Have someone drill the hole with an electric drill with a ⅝" spade bit and cut the mouth with a band saw.

Draw a Centerline

Use a ruler to find the center of the frog. Draw a centerline all around the frog to use as a reference.

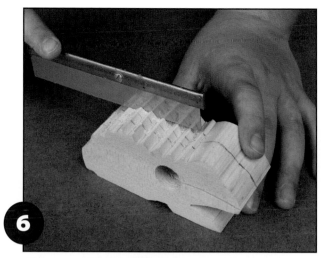

Measure and Cut the Sides

Across the back, ribbed area, measure over ¼" on both sides of the centerline. Use a backsaw to cut down to the depth of the ribs on both sides of the ribbed area. The ribs should be ½" wide.

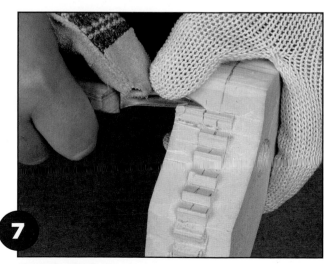

Carve the Back

Put on a carving glove and a thumb guard, and using a fixed-blade knife, carefully remove wood from both sides of the ribs using push cuts and pull cuts.

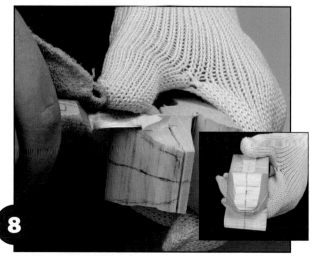

Draw and Round the Head

Draw the shape of the head so it's balanced on both sides. Then, round the head with the knife.

Making: Frog

9

Round the Face
Round the top of the face with the knife.

10

Shape the Eye Area
Working on your carving table, use a #9 ⅜" gouge to remove wood at the top of the head between the eyes.

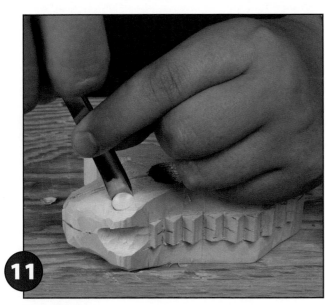

11

Carve the Eyes
With the gouge, use plunge cuts to form the eyes.

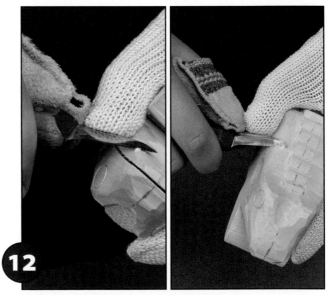

12

Round the Jaw and the Body
Put on the carving glove and thumb guard. With the knife, use push cuts and pull cuts to round the bottom of the jaw and then the body.

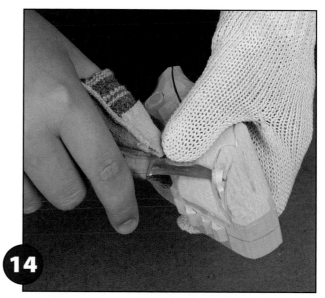

Cut the Back Legs

Use a V-tool to cut in the back legs. Then, use the gouge to remove wood from around the legs so they stick out farther than the frog's body.

Round the Legs

Round and shape the legs using the knife. Be sure to wear your carving glove and thumb guard.

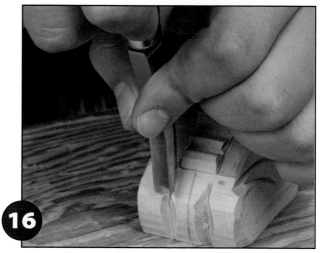

Make Stop Cuts

Use your backsaw to make stop cuts to shape the back of the legs.

Shape the Back Legs

Remove wood with the V-tool to shape the back legs.

Projects

Making: Frog

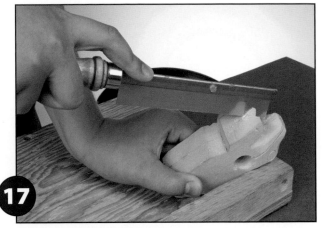

17

Separate the Front Legs
With the backsaw, cut between the front legs to separate them. Then, use the knife to shape them.

18

Sand
Sand the surface of the frog with 220- and then 320-grit sandpaper. Clean the surface of your carving before painting.

19

Paint the Frog
Paint the frog and the dowel. After the green and black paints dry, spray the surface with a gloss varnish. Frogs look wet, and the gloss varnish will give your frog a wet look. (Follow the manufacturer's instructions when using spray paint.)

20

Test the Frog
Hold the frog by its legs, and stroke the dowel across the ribbed back to make the croaking sound. For storage, the ⅝" dowel will fit in the hole drilled through the frog.

Glossary

This glossary has some terms you will find in the book's text and are listed again here for speedy reference. There are also new terms you might read or hear when learning more about woodcarving.

Hardwood: Wood that comes from deciduous trees, or trees whose leaves fall off in autumn.

Softwood: Wood that comes from coniferous trees, or trees with needles that stay on year-round.

Pith: The ring in the center of the tree. It's usually softer and darker than the rest of the wood.

Heartwood: Vessels in the middle of the tree that are not alive, but give strength to the tree. Heartwood develops when the entire trunk of the tree is not needed to carry water to the leaves anymore.

Cambium: The layer of the tree where cells divide and the tree grows. The cambium is found between the wood and bark.

Knot: A defect in a tree found where a limb broke off. Knots are hard and difficult to carve.

Grain: The arrangement of vessels in wood. Under a microscope, the grain looks like straws running through the wood.

Finishing: Treating the wood with a type of coat or covering after you've finished carving. Finishes include colored pencils, markers, wax, paint, and varnish.

Varnish: A type of finish. Varnish is transparent and is applied to protect the wood surface.

Square: A tool used to measure right (90º) angles. Many squares can also measure other angles, such as 45º angles.

Clamp: A tool that holds objects in place or holds them together. Most clamps have sliding or adjustable jaws that can be adjusted to fit the size of your project.

Pull cut: A type of cut that is frequently used in carving. Performing a pull cut is similar to peeling an apple.

Push cut: Another type of cut. The push cut is performed in the opposite direction of the pull cut.

Gouge: A tool with a curved cutting blade. The curve of the blade is called the sweep of the gouge.

V-tool: A tool with a V-shaped cutting edge. V-tools are used to make decorative cuts and outline carvings.

Strop: A hard surface covered with honing compound used to sharpen tools.

Honing compound: An abrasive that sharpens and polishes the blades of cutting tools.

Resources

Chipping Away, Inc.
General inquiries: 519-743-9008
Order line: 888-682-9801
www.chippingaway.com
(Carving tools, wood, roughouts)

The Woodcraft Shop
2724 State Street
Bettendorf, IA 52722
800-397-2278
www.thewoodcraftshop.com
(Everything for the woodcarver)

Moore Roughouts
P.O. Box 193
Kindred, ND 58051
800-825-2657
www.roughouts.com
(More than 500 roughouts available)

Wood Carvers Supply, Inc.
P.O. Box 7500
Englewood, FL 34295
800-284-6229
www.woodcarverssupply.com
(Woodcarving supplies—over 4000 products)

Woodcraft Supply, Inc.
210 Wood County Industrial Park
P.O. Box 1686
Parkersburg, WV 26102
800-225-1153
www.woodcraft.com
(Quality woodcarving tools and supplies)